When Ministry Hurts

When Ministry Hurts

Triumphalism and the Crisis of Trauma among Clergy

DALE SCOTT SANGER

WIPF & STOCK · Eugene, Oregon

WHEN MINISTRY HURTS
Triumphalism and the Crisis of Trauma among Clergy

Copyright © 2024 Dale Scott Sanger. All rights reserved. Except for brief quotations in critical publications or reviews, no part of this book may be reproduced in any manner without prior written permission from the publisher. Write: Permissions, Wipf and Stock Publishers, 199 W. 8th Ave., Suite 3, Eugene, OR 97401.

Wipf & Stock
An Imprint of Wipf and Stock Publishers
199 W. 8th Ave., Suite 3
Eugene, OR 97401

www.wipfandstock.com

PAPERBACK ISBN: 979-8-3852-1789-2
HARDCOVER ISBN: 979-8-3852-1790-8
EBOOK ISBN: 979-8-3852-1791-5

11/22/24

To my wife, Teresa —
who encouraged me along this journey and gave me her love and support during my educational endeavours. I could not have done it without you.

To my girls, Eden, Emily, and Charis —
I love you more than words can express. Keep seeking to know Jesus in deeper and more meaningful ways.

To my son, Dawson —
you are forever in my heart, and I look forward to seeing you in the coming Kingdom.

To my friend, Steve —
You have fought the good fight, you have finished the race.

Contents

List of Illustrations/Tables		ix
Introduction		xi
1	Why Look at Trauma among Clergy?	1
2	Trauma Studies & Theological Analysis	16
3	Research Methodology and Design	43
4	The Essence of Trauma in Pentecostal Clergy	60
5	The Trauma and Triumph of the Cross	94
6	Conclusion	125
Appendix One: List of Essences and Spiritual Practices		133
Appendix Two: Interview Guide		135
Appendix Three: McMaster Research Ethics Board		137
Appendix Four: Lament Worksheet—Psalms 13		139
Bibliography		141
Index		147

List of Illustrations/Tables

Figure 1—Human Function Curve	24
Figure 2—Essence Percentage vs Document Appearances	56
Figure 3—Significant Essences of Trauma	57
Figure 4—Essences of Trauma Graph	57
Figure 5—Phenomenological Description Summary Chart	83
Figure 6—Spiritual Practices Chart	84
Figure 7—Code System	133
Figure 8—Mcmaster Ethics Review Board Clearance	137
Figure 9—Lament Worksheet	139

Introduction

THIS BOOK WAS CONCEIVED first as a dissertation for my doctoral dissertation at McMaster Divinity College in Hamilton, Ontario. It was research based on my own experience with trauma and my Pentecostal theology and praxis, which means it is from a Practice–led Research model. While it is Canadian and Pentecostal in scope, I believe much can be applied to the wider Western church, whether they be Pentecostal or not.

Chapter 1 serves as an overview of the book, giving the reader a roadmap for where the book will travel. It also discusses why I would choose to look at trauma among clergy as a research topic. It outlines the need for trauma studies, gives a brief overview of the research methodology of Phenomenology, discusses Pentecostal triumphalism, and provides a first glimpse at Luther and his *theologia crucis* (Theology of the Cross). Finally, it provides the first look at lament as a spiritual practice. Chapter 1 serves as the skeleton for what the book will become when flesh is added.

Chapter 2 serves as a literature review for various subjects in the book. There is an intensive look at the modern field of trauma studies as championed by Charcot in the 19th century, culminating in looking at modern experts. A deep examination of the Phenomenology of Max Van Manen is undertaken to understand the research interview methodology. Then a look at Pentecostal theology is examined through both a historical and theological lens. After Pentecostal theology is examined, we then look at the theology of the reformer Martin Luther, specifically his *theologia crucis*. Finally, we look at the idea of lament as a spiritual practice through eyes of Luther, Walter Brueggeman, and others.

Chapter 3 is solely focused on the research methodology and design of the research. This is an important chapter for the person who wants a

Introduction

fuller understanding of the process used to examine the interview experiences, especially for the academic. For those less interested in this section, I suggest skipping and proceeding to Chapter 4, returning to Chapter 3 later if you want a fuller understanding of the process.

Chapter 4 is where the experiences of the interview subjects are brought to the forefront. With the use of quotes, the book highlights the experiences of the clergy members who have experienced trauma, and it presents the seven main "essences" of trauma. It is here where the reader can see the heart of the people who were the subjects of the interviews.

Chapter 5 looks at the experience of the research participants and examines the deficiencies of Pentecostal theology and praxis when dealing with trauma. It then brings into view the Lutheran ideals of *theologia crucis* and discusses how that theology can and should be implemented in the Pentecostal church. It shows that the Theology of the Cross is a good conversation partner for Pentecostals, and I then suggest that an ideal way to aid in this process is through the practice of lament both in an individual way and a corporate one. The chapter discusses how to incorporate both the theology and the practice of lament into the existing Pentecostal ethos.

Chapter 6 summarizes the book and discusses limitations discovered while researching and areas where future study might be beneficial.

1

Why Look at Trauma among Clergy?

WHILE PREPARING TO WRITE this chapter, I received a text message from a member of my church who asked if I could go for coffee. While this seems like a mundane request, for a pastor who has experienced trauma surrounding dissatisfied congregants, it immediately caused a sense of panic to rise within me. I have had congregants shout at me during annual business meetings, meet with me in private to express that they do not think I am good at being a pastor, others have stood over me at a board meeting and shoved their finger in my face while yelling, and a myriad of other actions that lead to a sense of dread, when what otherwise might be considered a mundane request comes in. All of this has caused my spiritual life to suffer. It causes me to wonder where God is in all of this. Has he not called me to be a pastor? Thus, I tend to shut down from both spiritual and social engagement during those times. Chapter 1 serves as a roadmap for the reasoning behind the book and where it will go in the following chapters.

This book's impetus arises from my experiences as a Pentecostal clergy member who has faced personal trauma and looks at trauma within two Canadian Pentecostal traditions. However, I believe that there is much in this work that applies to much of Christendom, especially in traditions that tend towards triumphalism. In many Christian theological circles, especially in Pentecostal circles, the person who has the role of pastor is the one who is supposed to have the spiritual answers, and so this shutdown is counterintuitive to the position they hold. These experiences and their representative responses are common in pastoral ministry. They highlight the significant trauma the person in religious ministry carries with them and emphasize the need for a theological belief system that allows them to understand their trauma and a spiritual praxis that aids in treating it.

The challenge for Pentecostal pastors is that they have an underlying theology of glory which does not appropriately consider personal trauma. The inherent properties of a theology of glory suggest that the sufferer seeks blessing to counter pain. If Pentecostals experience pain, it is considered to be not from God but rather a tool of Satan; this may cause the Pentecostal pastor to attempt to seek resolution through claiming blessings and cursing the pain associated with the trauma, which is not a healthy outlook, so Pentecostals, and the wider church, need a fuller understanding of trauma.[1] So that the Pentecostal pastor may be better prepared to deal with trauma, there first needs to be an addition to existing Pentecostal theology by incorporating Martin Luther's theology of the cross. Luther's theology of the cross, or *theologia crucis*, will allow Pentecostals to better understand Christ in His suffering and aid in their spiritual praxis with the inclusion of lament, which Luther utilized as part of his theology.

This book engages in primary research to better understand the spiritual practices of pastors who have experienced personal trauma; through engagement with the sociological conversation partner of trauma studies, an examination of the prevalence of trauma in the clergy is completed; this will allow the exploration of theological and spiritual strategies to help the sufferer understand what they are encountering while in trauma. The research utilizes a phenomenological interview process with eleven pastors who have in the past or are currently experiencing personal trauma. Interviews with people who fit these criteria allowed the researcher to document their trauma experiences and spiritual responses to them. Also, an examination of the Pentecostal theology of glory is completed to better understand its strengths and weaknesses. Cataloging Pentecostal theology allows for a better examination of it and will help in understanding where there needs to be an additive to their theology, namely the theology of the cross; doing this allows for a more holistic theology for the person suffering trauma. Exploration of the Christian practice of lament as understood by

---

1. Torr, *Dramatic*, 77–78, 209. Torr discussed Katherine Kuhlman's concepts of always being victorious or always able to have victory through Christ in pages 77–78. On page 209, he shares that Pentecostalism tends to "blame the sufferer for not claiming their healing, or to passively accept that God knows what he is doing."

WHY LOOK AT TRAUMA AMONG CLERGY?

Luther and described in scripture will reveal how this theology and praxis can benefit the pastor.[2]

DEFINING TRAUMA STUDIES?

Trauma studies is a field within psychology which explores the effects of traumatic situations on the human subject. Trauma is not the event, such as a car accident, but rather the "response generated when our capacity to adapt is overwhelmed."[3] While post-traumatic stress disorder (PTSD) is often the first condition that comes to mind when a person mentions the word trauma, it is not the only trauma-related condition. *The Diagnostic and Statistical Manual of Mental Disorders* (DSM-5) reveals five disorders related to trauma and related stressors. There are also associated disorders from other areas of study which align significantly with trauma-related conditions.[4]

French neurologist Jean-Martin Charcot championed trauma studies in the late nineteenth century, which were then characterized as hysteria studies. Prior to this, studies of hysteria were considered "beyond pale of serious scientific investigation."[5] Charcot, however, saw a field that needed serious research and would put hysteria patients on display by utilizing them in his live demonstrations. These live demonstrations by Charcot and his notoriety brought respectability to the previously much-despised and neglected study area. The new-found respectability led many practitioners to seek out Charcot; these included noted psychiatrists of his day, including Pierre Janet, William James, and Sigmund Freud.

---

2. While Luther's understanding of lament is primary, attention will also be given to the practice of lament in the church both historically and in modern contexts so that its full value to the pastor, and the church universal, may be better understood.

3. Grosch-Miller, *Trauma and Pastoral Care*, 11.

4. American Psychiatric Association and American Psychiatric Association, eds., *Diagnostic and Statistical Manual of Mental Disorders*, 265. The DSM-5 lists the five trauma and stressor related disorders as, reactive attachment disorder, disinhibited social engagement disorder, post-traumatic stress disorder, acute stress disorder, and adjustment disorder. They also note that the placement of the chapter on trauma and stressors in relation to the chapters around it is intentional as it reveals that there is a close association between these disorders and the disorders related to anxiety, obsessive-compulsive and related disorders, as well as adjustment disorders.

5. Herman, *Trauma and Recovery*, 10.

Both Freud and Janet realized psychological trauma brought on "altered states of consciousness."[6] In essence, trauma studies found that there was a dissociation from reality to cope with the traumatic life events, which can cause the actions of the person facing trauma to be drastically different from their usual pattern of behaviour. Change occurs in the behaviour of the traumatized because trauma affects our capacity to adapt to the situations around us, and we rely instead on our more primal instincts. The DSM-5 reveals these primal instincts as it lists the prominent clinical characteristics of trauma disorders. It suggests they are "anhedonic and dysphoric symptoms, externalizing angry and aggressive symptoms, or dissociative symptoms."[7] The research of Charcot, Freud, Janet, and others helped to reveal that the symptoms associated with hysteria could be alleviated when the patients would recover the traumatic memories into active memory and relay the intense emotions that accompanied those memories into words. This synergy between reawakening the memories and the emotions that accompanied them allowed psychiatrists to explore a new range of prescriptive ideas for treating the traumatized individual.

The early twentieth century saw the rise of the study of war-related trauma, which arose due to the horrors of trench warfare of the First World War. British psychologist Charles Myers, who had examined some of the first cases, coined the term "shell shock" even though it quickly became apparent that war trauma effects were not limited to those who had endured the exploding of shells around them.[8] From the late twentieth century until today, one of the premier practitioners in trauma is Bessel Van der Kolk.[9] Dr. Van der Kolk has been noted as one of the leading authorities on PTSD (Post-traumatic Stress Disorder).[10] The work of Van der Kolk is utilized in this book so that a modern understanding of trauma and its effects can be seen.

---

6. Herman, *Trauma and Recovery*, 12.

7. American Psychiatric Association and American Psychiatric Association, eds., *Diagnostic and Statistical Manual of Mental Disorders*, 265.

8. Herman, *Trauma and Recovery*, 20.

9. Grosch-Miller, *Trauma and Pastoral Care*, 14.

10. Schiraldi, *Post-Traumatic Stress Disorder Sourcebook*, 236.

THE RELEVANCE OF TRAUMA STUDIES FOR THE PASTOR

It was December 2019 when Canadians began to see reports of a virus in a city in China that most probably had never heard of before. Here was yet another news story about an event on the other side of the planet that most people assumed would not affect their lives. However, that view would soon change over the next few months. In March 2020, the virus spread beyond the city of Wuhan, China and took hold worldwide. The once-isolated virus was now spreading and was the cause of a worldwide traumatic event. This event has affected every person in Canada in one way or another.

A worldwide pandemic is one extreme case of a traumatic event, but many other events are smaller in scale and less far-reaching but still cause trauma to the person experiencing them. There are major traumas such as COVID-19, sexual assault, 9/11, and so-called more minor traumas such as bullying and verbal abuse, which are less violent or global in nature, yet just as traumatic. Since trauma is more pervasive in our society than many comprehend, including those in active pastoral ministry, we must examine it freshly, as this book hopes to do, and apply corrective measures to our spiritual practices. Mineela Chand, a Licensed Marriage and Family Therapist with the state of Pennsylvania, suggests that traumatic events "change how you think about yourself, the world, and your relationships which carry a negative connotation."[11] It can then be surmised that trauma affects people in all strata of life. So, it should be of no surprise that clergy are also affected by personal trauma and vicarious and secondary trauma. Vicarious trauma has diverse symptoms and results from the caregiver having multiple and ongoing exposures to another person's trauma. Secondary trauma on the other hand is when the caregiver starts experiencing the symptoms of the person they are caring for.[12] This vicarious and secondary trauma worsens traumatic reactions when the clergy also experience personal trauma.

It should also be noted that clergy are in a category of caregivers, which includes first responders, who often have delayed traumatic reactions. Judith Herman posits that these delayed reactions, common among the clergy, can manifest themselves through various symptoms including, but not limited to, "unrelenting fatigue, sleep disorders, nightmares, fear of

---

11. Chand, Mineela, Zoom Meeting, February 17, 2021.
12. Grosch-Miller, *Trauma and Pastoral Care*, 53.

recurrence, anxiety focussed on flashbacks, depression and avoidance of emotions."[13] These manifestations will disrupt the routine of life and can even affect spiritual practices.

The marks of trauma on the person are not always apparent. There may not be a scar or a missing limb, but the effects of trauma find a residence in the human mind and emotions. This results in compromised relationships and an inability to adapt to and cope with situations. Bessel Van der Kolk posits that the result of trauma on the human mind and emotion is an adverse reaction to "our capacity for joy and intimacy, and even on our biology and immune systems."[14] It must be understood that trauma affects every area of our lives as pastors, from our relationships with family, congregation members, community, and even our relationship with God. Trauma pushes the person into a sense of dual reality, the relatively secure present and the devasting ever-present past. According to Van der Kolk, the essence of trauma is "overwhelming, unbelievable, and unbearable. Each patient demands that we suspend our sense of what is normal and accept that we are dealing with a dual reality."[15] Pastors who do not understand and confront their trauma will be stuck in a different reality, affecting every aspect of their lives, including their spiritual practices. The usage of trauma studies in this book aids in bringing to light the realities of trauma as experienced by clergy.

DESIGN AND METHODOLOGY

This book utilizes several methods. These methods include practice-led research as seen through the lens of practical theology, trauma studies, theological deliberation, and lament as a spiritual practice. Each of these will be detailed more fully in this section.

Practice-led Research and the Practical Theology Lens

The overall research structure for this project is practice-led research. It forms the basis of the inquiry at hand, and the problem is one that I, as the researcher, have faced firsthand. As the researcher, I study as one in

---

13. Grosch-Miller, *Trauma and Pastoral Care*, 18.
14. Van der Kolk, *Body Keeps*, 1.
15. Van der Kolk, *Body Keeps*, 197.

practice utilizing my expertise, not as one outside of the practice, which is the model traditional doctoral research often implements. Neil Ferguson aptly observes practice-led research "is investigating a problem that has arisen within practice or as a part of an individual's practice. In other words, the issue appears as a result of their practice and would not be seen outside that practice."[16] Practical theology can examine the lived experience of those who suffer trauma, especially as it concerns their spiritual practices. Warner et al. posit that those who study trauma "have been able to refine the response to trauma by focusing on the lived experience of it, so too a focus on the lived experience of trauma aids the theologians in their task of speaking of God. The theological discipline particularly well suited to working with human experience is Practical Theology."[17] Since Practical Theology is well suited as a conversation partner, it will be used to evaluate this research and provide a theological perspective to the existing literature on trauma.

This project comes through the researcher's practice as a Pentecostal clergy member for over thirty years. In this role, I am responsible for my spiritual well-being and direction regarding the spirituality of others in my care. I have found that personal traumatic experiences have, at times, led to a crisis of faith, which my Pentecostal theology has not adequately equipped me to navigate. Using trauma studies as a lens allowed me to explore my trauma and give me coping strategies. The phenomenological interviews revealed a reality that Pentecostal clergy often have trauma as an unwanted influence in their lives, and this affects their spiritual praxis, which then can affect their family, friends, and congregation. The essence of practical theology is to gather and utilize the evidence to imagine a better way. The research will help us look for a better way through the insights from the reflections of those who have experienced trauma, the addition of Luther's theology of the cross into Pentecostal theology, and the practice of lament as a spiritual practice for the pastor, which is examined later in this book.

Life is like a calm river, and life continues merrily down the same path while the water slowly erodes the banks, a process we do not see. However, eventually, a storm brews or the river is blocked, and this causes the water of life to make more drastic changes to the environment. The landscape is re-formed with its surge, and new paths are made. Practical theology seeks to guide through both the micro and macro changes of life. Using practical

---

16. Ferguson, "Practice-Led Theology," 119.
17. Ison, "Embodied and Systemic," 11.

theology allows for gathering tools that will aid in interpreting the praxis. Practical theology wishes to discern what is happening by interpreting what is. Therefore, practical theology "seeks to recognize, describe, identify, and understand the context before it."[18] This is achieved by harnessing multiple approaches, sociological, psychological, theological, or whatever tools are needed to determine what is happening in the lives of the research participants. The tools utilized in this book include trauma studies, spiritual praxis, and theology. A better way forward is proposed so we can find a solution to the problem presented while remaining faithful to God. As Cahalan and Nieman share of this process, "practical theology does not offer ideological proposals for optimistic progress, but theological ones aimed at new forms of faithful service that take risks within our own time and place."[19] Trauma and its effects on the spirituality of the clergyperson are studied in this book, and through practical theology, a reimagining of Pentecostal praxis to include the ancient practice of lament as understood through the *theologia crucis* is proposed.

Theological Studies

There exists a tension between Pentecostal theology and the Pentecostal who is suffering. Pentecostals have historically held a theological perspective which is highly triumphalist. David Courey states that the problem with Pentecostal theology is that it has become one of triumphalism, which has become "endemic to Pentecostalism."[20] He goes on to say that the "unwritten measure of true Spirit-fullness among Pentecostals is not so much speaking in tongues, as it is indomitable faith: the confident assertion that, whatever the circumstance, God will come through; and, its necessary corollary for the Pentecostal, by faith I will overcome."[21] This primarily occurs due to the focus on Spirit empowerment which stresses equally the "power encounters over the dark forces in personal healing, ecstatic tongues, and a sense of triumph in the Spirit over all that opposes the will of God."[22] Pentecostals emphasize God's sovereign power, evidenced by the presence of the Holy Spirit and a personal experience of Christ through that same Spirit.

18. Cahalan and Nieman, "Mapping the Field," 82.
19. Cahalan and Nieman, "Mapping the Field," 84.
20. Courey, *What Has Wittenberg*, 4.
21. Courey, *What Has Wittenberg*, 71.
22. Macchia, *Baptized*, 233.

Within Pentecostal circles, there is a strong belief that "there are binding, hindering forces and systems in this world which threaten to smother the life out of them and to stifle their worship."²³ The crux of this work is to discuss the addition of Luther's theology of the cross to the existing Pentecostal theology; this is done not to be adversarial towards the existing theology but to provide a fuller theology through the addition.

Luther's theology of the cross provides a place where we can interact with "God hidden in suffering."²⁴ Luther sees value in Christians embracing their suffering so that we may see God through it. Courey, a Pentecostal himself, argues for this addition and sees that through embracing a more robust theology of the cross, Pentecostals will find their suffering and trauma as a place where God is revealed. Our cross, as manifested in our trauma, then becomes for us "the place of divine revelation."²⁵ These ideas are explored more deeply in chapter 2, and then the integration of the theologies into praxis is considered more in chapter 5.

Lament as a Spiritual Practice

Walter Brueggemann asks, "What happens when appreciation of the lament as a form of speech and faith is lost, as I think it is largely lost in contemporary usage?"²⁶ Brueggemann's quote highlights the absence of the usage of lament in most contemporary Christian circles. Soong-Chan Rah writes, "The American church avoids lament. Consequently, the underlying narrative of suffering that requires lament is lost in lieu of a triumphalistic, victorious narrative. We forget the necessity of lament over suffering and pain."²⁷ The Canadian Pentecostal church is no different from the American churches Rah describes. Yes, we allow for grieving; however, it is often compartmentalized and put out of sight, save for the days surrounding the funeral or a significant accident. We have relegated lament to historical Christianity's dust

---

23. Richie and Land, *Essentials*, 101.
24. Luther, "Heidelberg Disputation (1518)."
25. Courey, *What Has Wittenberg*, 166.
26. Brueggemann, *Life of Faith*, 102.
27. Rah, "Absence of Lament." In this article, Rah provides the statistics for several American denomination hymnbooks as well as the Christian Copyright License International (CCLI) data of the top worship songs utilized by churches in the year prior to printing. He noted that the Psalms were approximately 40 percent lament, while the highest percentage of hymns which could be considered lament used by a denomination was only 19 percent.

bins and downgraded them from our corporate expression in worship. The church, as John Swinton declares, "remains in denial, excluding the reality of pain and evil."[28] Perhaps we move away from lament because we do not want to be reminded of the pain and suffering we are experiencing and would instead shuttle these feelings off to the far reaches of our memory. Lament, which is expressed, however, can spur "movement towards God at a time when natural instinct is to move away from God. Lament gives a voice to rage and releases us to experience God's compassion."[29] Our voices raised, even in anger, toward God can help us start a healing process when facing trauma. Sigmund Freud and his mentor Josef Breuer brought a similar idea when they utilized a process they christened "the talking cure."[30] In a paper published in 1893, Freud and Breuer noticed a marked improvement in patients who had undertaken the talking cure.

Similarly, in lament, we talk out our trauma with God, even if it is expressed in a way that draws into question the motives of God. The psalmist utilizes this methodology when he inquires of God, "How long, Lord? Will you forget me forever? How long will you hide your face from me? How long must I wrestle with my thoughts and day after day have sorrow in my heart? How long will my enemy triumph over me?" (Ps 13:1–2 NIV).

A lament is an act of crying out in faith to God. It is not neat and tidy; it is not an idyllic image but rather a messy and hellish picture of the realities of life as it is lived. It is in these moments that we cry out to God. As Colin Buchanan suggests, our lament may involve "crying out against God, of anger against God, of puzzlement–aporia–in the presence of God, but all expressions are done with the knowledge that God. . .is nevertheless there, and in liturgy being specifically addressed."[31] The reinsertion of lament into the spiritual practices of the Pentecostal clergy will also help the congregation see the value of lament, which will bring a renewed vibrancy in congregational worship. Miller–McLemore declares that pastoral theology has a strong legacy of "investigating human suffering and spiritual recovery, creating fresh theological loci such as pain, lament, and joy."[32] The background of lament will be discussed in chapter 2, and the idea of its usage in Pentecostal praxis is discussed further in chapter 5.

28. Swinton, *Raging with Compassion*, 113.
29. Swinton, *Raging with Compassion*, 113.
30. Van der Kolk, *Body Keeps*, 184.
31. Buchanan, "Liturgy and Lament," 157.
32. Miller-McLemore, *Christian Theology*, 18.

Phenomenological Interview Methodology

This book arose out of my doctoral studies. Prior to conducting research with living participants, the project was evaluated by the McMaster Research Ethics Board (MREB), and guidelines were established to protect the privacy and mental health of the participants. This research followed those guidelines, and a copy of the approval from the MREB is available in Appendix 3.

Van Manen describes phenomenology as a "project of sober reflection on the lived experience of human existence–sober, in the sense that reflecting on experience must be thoughtful, and as much as possible, free from theoretical, prejudicial and suppositional intoxications."[33] Van Manen continues suggesting that phenomenology is also driven by a fascination with the researcher being "swept up in a spell of wonder, a fascination with meaning."[34] Essentially, phenomenology allows the phenomena to reveal themselves through observation.

The data for this book was gathered using phenomenological interviews. Through this, an exploration of the phenomenon of pastors experiencing trauma who perceive an absence of God's presence or other essences of trauma was undertaken to examine its effect on their spirituality.[35] In phenomenological interviews, two broad questions are asked. "What have you experienced in terms of the phenomenon? What contexts or situations have typically influenced or affected your experiences of the phenomenon?"[36] Therefore, the two specific questions were, "How has trauma impacted your relationship with God and your spiritual disciplines?" and "What steps do you take to address this feeling?" Other open-ended questions were also used to understand better their concept of the phenomenon.

Phenomenology and practical theology are known to both "share the importance of expression or vocalizing a concrete experience."[37] This makes phenomenology best suited as the method of understanding the experiences of the pastors interviewed for this study. Campbell declares that phenomenology in the study of suffering is being used by scholars so that "we may articulate suffering as lived, embodied experience."[38] Therefore,

---

33. Van Manen, "Phenomenology of Practice," 11.
34. Van Manen, "Phenomenology of Practice," 11.
35. Creswell and Poth, *Qualitative Inquiry*, 76.
36. Creswell and Poth, *Qualitative Inquiry*, 79.
37. Zylla, "Shades of Lament," 765.
38. Campbell, "Glory in Suffering?," 520.

the embodied experience of trauma in the pastor's life has been brought into view through phenomenology so that it can be explored by both the researcher and the research participant.

Phenomenology is known to have a robust philosophical aspect, drawing on the writing of mathematician Edmund Husserl.[39] The phenomenological question is the gateway to understanding the phenomenon. The researcher must ask themselves. "How do we form the question that makes the basis of our Phenomenological research?" Truls Åkerlund shows that "The foundational question asked in phenomenological inquiry is that of meaning, structure, and essence of the lived experience of this phenomenon for a person or group, and aims for a deeper and fuller understanding of what it is like for someone to experience something."[40] The aim then is to understand the meaning of an experience through the eyes of the person who experienced it, without the "theoretical overlay that might be put on it by the researcher, and to provide a comprehensive and rich description of it."[41] This methodology will allow the research to probe deep into the lived experience of the interviewee so a more precise picture can emerge.

Max Van Manen's phenomenological practice will be relied upon for this study; he presents concepts in *Phenomenology of Practice* which will be utilized. First, he posits that phenomenological questions may cause us to pause and reflect. Even at the most ordinary experience, which will make us ask, what is this experience like?[42] Therefore, phenomenology and the phenomenological question are the backbones of the process. This project will perform a phenomenological interview whose aim is to gather "prereflective experiential accounts."[43] The dual-pronged purpose of phenomenological interviews is first to be used to gather and explore "experiential narrative material that may serve as a resource for developing a richer and deeper understanding of human phenomenon."[44] Second, the interview may help develop a "conversational relationship with a partner (interviewee) about the meaning of an experience."[45]

---

39. Creswell and Poth, *Qualitative Inquiry*, 75.
40. Akerlund, *Phenomenology of Pentecostal Leadership*, 6–7.
41. Swinton and Mowat, *Practical Theology*, 50.
42. Van Manen, *Phenomenology of Practice*, 31.
43. Van Manen, *Phenomenology of Practice*, 311.
44. Van Manen, *Researching Lived Experience*, 66.
45. Van Manen, *Researching Lived Experience*, 66.

Why Look at Trauma among Clergy?

Before any phenomenological study is undertaken, two steps must be completed: the *epoché* and the reduction.[46] The *epoché* is the opening of oneself so that you can set aside presuppositions. The reduction then flows from this process so that the researcher can view the phenomenon as it unfolds without bias. With these two items in place, the researcher can conduct the interviews, allowing thematizing and analysis to take place.[47]

Van Manen warns that any analysis of recollections of experiences, no matter which way the data is collected, is already a "transformation of those experiences."[48] The interview subjects will have already transformed what they experienced to see it through their lens of perception. As the interview is conducted and later codified, the researcher asks themselves, "How does this speak to the phenomenon?"[49] So, even in the study of the interviews, there is a further transformation of the experience.

Phenomenologists borrow the experiences of others, not just to gather data as many methods do, but so that we can "collect examples of possible human experiences in order to reflect on the meanings that may inhere in them."[50] The phenomenological interview does not ask the subject's views, interpretations, or opinions about their trauma; instead, the interview seeks to understand the phenomenon of trauma as they experienced it, to understand the effects it had on their being in a deeper sense than just analysis of that which caused the trauma.

Seven pointers, as laid out by Van Manen were utilized for the interview process, which details the "Where, Who, When, Why, How, What, and Whatever" during the interviews.[51] Following these steps was believed to give the participants a better chance of feeling comfortable sharing their stories. After achieving comfort between the interviewer and interviewee, it was easier to center on the topic and ask specific questions about the phenomenon. These methods allowed the interview to remain focused on the central question and remain unstructured in format. In doing this, the interviewee could move the experience naturally from their memory to their words. Swinton and Mowat describe this process of unstructured

---

46. Van Manen, *Phenomenology of Practice*, 216–18.
47. Van Manen, *Phenomenology of Practice*, 312.
48. Van Manen, *Phenomenology of Practice*, 313.
49. Van Manen, *Phenomenology of Practice*, 312.
50. Van Manen, *Phenomenology of Practice*, 313.
51. Van Manen, *Phenomenology of Practice*, 315–16.

interviews and were "deemed most likely to elicit rich data that would enable participants freely to relate their personal narratives."[52]

Following the interviews, the data was analyzed using the lifeworld technique and thematic analysis of Van Manen, which is given in more detail in chapters 3 and 4.

Recruitment of Participants

Participants were recruited through various methods. First and foremost, an invitation and a letter of information about the study were published on a private Facebook group for Pentecostal Assemblies of Canada and Pentecostal Assemblies of Newfoundland and Labrador pastors. The interested people were instructed to contact the researcher to obtain more information. Everyone who contacted the researcher was screened to ensure that they met the eligibility requirements as put forward in the Letter of Information, which can be found online.[53] The second method utilized to recruit participants was through referrals by other pastors for someone they thought may be qualified for the study. The same letter of information was sent to these possible candidates. As was done with the first recruitment method, this group was also screened to ensure eligibility.

Confidentiality and Data Analysis

Each interview was approximately one hour in length and was conducted via a secure Zoom connection; the video and audio were recorded.[54] The interviews were transferred in two password-protected USB drives. After the interviews were transcribed, coded, and a confirmation with the participants had taken place, the videos were deleted and all identifying elements in the interviews were scrubbed to ensure confidentiality.[55]

The transcribed interviews were analyzed in two ways to find any common themes. First, a manual analysis was done, and each interview's

---

52. Swinton and Mowat, *Practical Theology*, 55.

53. https://www.dropbox.com/sh/qpio5zq34ookezg/AABzR6qHBSMRtrwU6_oxC69Ba?dl=0

54. A second interview which was shorter in nature was completed prior to deletion of the videos and after coding to ensure that the researcher comprehended what the participant was sharing. This also acts as a verification of findings of the data.

55. These elements include but are not limited to: name, age, location, and gender.

themes were documented. Next an automated analysis was done using the program MAXQDA. This software allowed the researcher to see items such as common word usage in single interviews and between interviews and discover common themes in the interviews and areas of divergence.

Research Project Overview

This book has four components. The literature review in chapter 2 examines several key areas. First, trauma studies are explored to reveal the impact trauma has on the human psyche and examine the treatments for trauma disorders that have been utilized in the mental health field. It also reveals that trauma is widespread and also the cause of other illnesses in our society. The study of trauma in chapter 2 helps us better understand why even pastors can be affected by it.

The literature review then secondly focuses on the theological component of the study. A broad look at Pentecostal theology and the study of Martin Luther's theology of the cross is undertaken. The study of Pentecostal theology was completed to show that there is an underlying theology of glory that results in triumphalism. Luther's theology is then examined so that it could be utilized and understood as an excellent addition to Pentecostal theology that will provide balance to the theology of glory. The final section in chapter 2 discusses the historical usage of lament, especially by Luther, as an act of worship.

Chapter 3 explores the data acquired through the interview process, and the coding criteria is set out. In addition, there has been an exploration of the core analytical tools used. The major themes, areas of agreement between the subjects, and areas of divergence have been examined in this chapter.

Chapter 4 summarizes and analyzes primary research arising through phenomenological interviews. The chapter ends with a detailed description of how PAOC and PAONL pastors deal with trauma concerning their general life and spiritual practices.

Throughout chapter 5, there is a dialogue between the PAOC and PAONL pastors who have experienced trauma and are exploring their spiritual practices. These are explored through the lens of Luther by utilizing his writings and the findings of other theologians as well.

Chapter 6, which is the final section of the book, discloses the limitations of the study and proposes areas of possible future research that may be undertaken.

2

Trauma Studies & Theological Analysis

THIS CHAPTER PROVIDES A foundation for this book by engaging relevant literature in several key areas. In part one, an examination surrounding the field of trauma studies occurs, this begins with an overview of the history of trauma studies. Doing this helps establish a foundation that reveals the scholarly contribution this area of study has provided and obtains a description and definition of trauma, which aids in cataloging the effects on the individual's physiological, psychological, and even spiritual praxis. Part one will also examine some common treatments of trauma as used by professionals in trauma research.

Pentecostals hold to a theology of glory, which affects their ability to deal with negative situations, especially trauma. In the second part of this chapter, Pentecostal theology and Pentecostal spiritual praxis are examined by looking at various Pentecostal theologians' work to discover aspects of Pentecostal theology that contribute to this theology of glory. This examination allows the historical and current trends in Pentecostal theology, especially related to the theology of glory, to be brought to the forefront.

Once the theology of glory is examined, the third part of the chapter looks at the Lutheran ideal of a theology of the cross. Luther's thoughts on the theology of the cross are examined, most notably through *The Heidelberg Disputation*. In addition, other Lutheran theologians' works that discuss the *theologia crucis* are examined. Pentecostal theologians who have already interacted with this specific theology of Luther are also considered in this section.

AN INTERACTION WITH TRAUMA STUDIES

The history of trauma studies is complicated; it has vacillated between moments of intense interest by professionals to seeming obscurity at other moments. The current trend to study trauma originated in the late-nineteenth century when noted French neurologist Jean-Marin Charcot began to study it anew. At the beginning of Charcot's work in the area, trauma was referred to as hysteria and was mainly associated with a condition that females primarily possessed. His studies in hysteria proved so influential that they enticed distinguished physicians such as Pierre Janet, William James, and Sigmund Freud to make the pilgrimage to the hospital in Paris where Charcot was conducting his revolutionary work. In her seminal work *Trauma and Recovery*, Judith Herman describes Charcot's influence on the study of trauma as renowned "not only in the world of medicine but also in the larger worlds of literature and politics."[1] It was Charcot's prestige and his voice which lent credibility to the then much-maligned study of hysteria. Through his studies and those of Freud, Breuer, Janet, and others, the study of trauma moved from being a condition considered only to affect women to revealing that it was a prevalent condition regardless of gender or age; trauma was shown to be far-reaching and invasive in its nature.

Events that cause trauma overwhelm the ability to adapt; however, those external events are not the actual experience of trauma; it is instead the human reaction to varied events that threaten the traumatized person's perceived safety. Warner et al. state, "It is now clear that trauma is not in an external event. Rather, it is a specific and automatic collection of physiological responses to an event, which are triggered when an individual's or community's adaptive capacity is overwhelmed."[2] The impairment of the person's capacity to adapt results in there being effects on all areas of their being. Trauma affects the brain and its ability to process, but it can define how genetic characteristics are passed from generation to generation and affect one's responses to dangerous stimuli in abnormal ways.[3]

---

1. Herman, *Trauma and Recovery*, 10.
2. Ison, "Embodied and Systemic," 1.
3. Conti, *Trauma*, 11, 14. Shows in this work that trauma can affect generations not only through direct contact with the traumatized person, but through genetic succession.

Trauma is not uncommon; it reaches into the majority of homes with events that can overwhelm the adaptation process of people experiencing it. Studies have shown that 70 percent of the population of the United States has experienced a form of personal trauma.[4] Judith Herman writes, "Traumatic events are extraordinary, not because they occur rarely, but because they overwhelm the ordinary human adaptations to life."[5] Paul Conti then surmises that trauma is not unique but that it affects everything, and "an alarming percentage of us has been significantly hurt in ways that can not be seen from the outside . . . By trauma, I'm referring to the type of emotional and physical pain that often goes unseen, yet actually changes our brain biology and psychology."[6] As described by Herman, the essence of what makes it extraordinary reveals the importance of trauma becoming better understood in our culture, the church, and the clergy. Because of the prevalence of trauma, it is essential to understand its effect on society and, for this study, the effects on Canadian Pentecostal clergy.

In a Canadian study of almost 3,000 people over eighteen, researchers found significant exposure to traumatic events among the populace. The research by Van Ameringen et al. shows that 76.1 percent of Canadians have experienced at least one traumatic event in their lifetime.[7] That study concluded that because a relatively large portion of the Canadian population has or will experience trauma in their lifetime, it can be considered a common occurrence. They also determined that while most within that group will find that the trauma will likely resolve itself, within the larger group, there is a 10 percent subset group "who appear to be particularly vulnerable and develop full syndromal PTSD. This disorder seems to have significant morbidity and impairment in social and occupational functioning and, along with its associated sequelae, is quite chronic in a large proportion of affected individuals."[8]

Judith Herman describes psychological trauma as "an affliction of the powerless. At the moment of trauma, the victim is rendered helpless by

---

Conti also posits that through genetics and our own life experience gives credence to the "multi-hit hypothesis" which states that our coping mechanisms are weakened by repeated traumatic experiences.

4. "How to Manage Trauma,"[n.d.], 1.
5. Herman, *Trauma and Recovery*, 33.
6. Conti, *Trauma*, 9.
7. Van Ameringen et al., "Post-Traumatic Stress Disorder," 177.
8. Van Ameringen et al., "Post-Traumatic Stress Disorder," 179.

overwhelming force."⁹ These overwhelming forces can cause the person experiencing the traumatic to feel defeated, which will cause the standard functions that provide systems for care to become less effective, which in turn will cause a loss of control, connection, and meaning for the person in trauma.

Physiologically, humanity is wired to react to trauma. Within the human brain lies two almond-shaped nuclei known as the amygdala, which become activated in response to trauma stimuli. These small clusters are responsible for processing whether a person is safe or not, which leads to a fight-or-flight response.[10] While all humans have the same physiology in their limbic system, which helps control traumatic responses, some people deal with the effects of the traumatic situations on their lives better than others. The typical response to a traumatic situation, especially a heinous one, is for individuals to want to bury those thoughts deep in their memory, in a place they will not readily access. Judith Herman states that all people wish to do the same thing in response to trauma, for the "ordinary response to atrocities is to banish them from consciousness."[11] Trauma, however, cannot be buried, for when a person tries to do that, it sets into motion the inner desire of the body to also proclaim it. The body proclaims it in various ways, including, but not limited to, physiological symptoms or emotional reactions that are not the normative ones for the individual. Although humanity desires to not live with the constant reminder of personal trauma, the body betrays that desire if trauma is not adequately addressed. Instead, the human body holds onto the traumatic events, which leave an indelible imprint.[12] While not always physically visible through scars or damage to the body, these imprints on the body are just as real as any physical impairment. Trauma leaves traces of itself on our "minds and emotions, on our capacity for joy and intimacy, and even on our biology and immune systems."[13]

9. Herman, *Trauma and Recovery*, 33.

10. Grosch-Miller, *Trauma and Pastoral Care*, 13. This section of Grosch-Miller's book explains the process of the flight or fight mechanism which is triggered in the brain when confronted with circumstances which pose danger for a person. She outlines that when a person is unable to either engage in flight or fight, that they may instead enter into a freeze or flop mentality which renders the individual unresponsive to the traumatic or threatening stimuli.

11. Herman, *Trauma and Recovery*, 1.

12. Grosch-Miller, *Trauma and Pastoral Care*, 8.

13. Van der Kolk, *The Body Keeps the Score*, 1.

Aside from the outward signs of inner trauma, internal and biological reactions are also caused by internalized traumatic events. These are triggered when something reminds the human mind of past traumatic events. A similar situation or a sensation can cause the mind to react as if the traumatic event were being experienced again, and the same responses as the original event can occur. Grosch-Miller calls this the imprint of traumatizing events "of which we may have no conscious memory. Triggered responses include a racing heartbeat; feelings of anxiety, threat, confusion or distress; a brain that has gone offline."[14] Conti categorizes these reactions by examining how trauma can be caused by discussing the four different ways a person will have a traumatic reaction: acute trauma, chronic trauma, vicarious trauma, and post-trauma syndromes.[15]

Acute trauma is often associated with a specific event or repeated events in which the individual loses their sense of well-being. Situations such as war, rape, abuse, and neglect are examples of this type of experience which causes a traumatic reaction. These severe events can trigger effects of "fear, pain, horror, intense vulnerability, and losing the illusion that we can predict or control life in such a way as to ward off disaster."[16] Herman's book discusses in full detail the subject of trauma; in it, she has a dedicated focus on the effects of abuse and terror on the traumatized person and reveals that the person who has undergone an acute traumatic situation is "usually extremely frightened and flooded with intrusive symptoms, such as nightmares and flashbacks."[17] This highlights a critical symptom which occurs in all forms of trauma, the anxiety the person experiences at the moment. Anxiety in the traumatized is the combination of "worrisome thoughts plus excessive emotional and physical arousal."[18] The anxiety of this type causes the body to stay in a state of hyperarousal, during which the mind stays vigilant and always on alert, which keeps the body in an aroused state. According to Schiraldi, anxiety accounts for bewildering symptoms, including physical, emotional, mental, and spiritual fatigue.[19] This hyperarousal can

---

14. Grosch-Miller, *Trauma and Pastoral Care*, 8.

15. Conti, *Trauma*. The author examines the four different methods that trauma is received in chapter 2 of his book.

16. Conti, *Trauma*, 19.

17. Herman, *Trauma and Recovery*, 218.

18. Schiraldi, *Post-Traumatic Stress Disorder Sourcebook*, 13.

19. Schiraldi, *Post-Traumatic Stress Disorder Sourcebook*, 14. When the effects of trauma on the pastor's spirituality are discussed later it is important to view the effects not just on the spiritual capacity but to incorporate the four areas that Schiraldi discusses

Trauma Studies & Theological Analysis

last a significant time, but according to Herman, after the acute traumatic situation occurs, a sense of safety can be generally restored "within a matter of weeks if adequate social support is available."[20]

Chronic trauma is the second type; unlike acute trauma, which is one significant and severe traumatic event, chronic trauma is characterized by prolonged exposure to harmful situations. Situations like ongoing racism, constant bullying, and ongoing sexual abuse are examples of chronic trauma. In essence, it is a prolonged experience that proves detrimental to the person's sense of safety and well-being. Conti explains that the symptoms of this type of trauma are often expressed in terms of "ongoing self-doubt, hopelessness, insecurity, fear, negativity about the world, and shame. Both acute and chronic trauma pave the way for shame, but chronic trauma allows shame to hide better."[21] The person's reactions to acute and chronic trauma are markedly unique. Herman explains that the person who experiences chronic trauma can develop a "progressive form of post-traumatic stress disorder that invades and erodes the personality. While the victim of a single acute trauma may feel after the event that she is "not herself," the victim of chronic trauma may feel herself to be changed irrevocably, or she may lose the sense that she has any self at all."[22] It is the wearing down of who the person is and the loss of identity which are the key symptoms of the person who experiences chronic trauma. Bessel Van der Kolk explains that traumatized people "chronically feel unsafe inside their bodies: The past is alive in the form of gnawing interior discomfort. Their bodies are constantly bombarded by visceral warning signs, and, in an attempt to control these processes, they often become experts at ignoring their gut feelings and in numbing awareness of what is playing out inside."[23] The traumatized person is hiding from themselves and instead painting a false reality to cope with their trauma. While that may seem acceptable, there is a price to this method as it does not allow the traumatized person to detect

---

since the traumatized is not a compartmentalized person. With physical fatigue the person experiences symptoms that can include but are not limited to tension, fatigue, and panic. Emotional fatigue can induce a feeling of irritation, moodiness, fear, and loss of confidence. Mental fatigue is marked by confusion, an inability of concentrate, remember, and make decisions. Finally spiritual fatigue can lead to discouragement, hopelessness, and despair. All four areas will receive triggering during anxiety.

20. Herman, *Trauma and Recovery*, 165.
21. Conti, *Trauma*, 20.
22. Herman, *Trauma and Recovery*, 86.
23. Van der Kolk, *Body Keeps*, 98–99.

what is truly dangerous and harmful to them, and equally, it does not allow them to realize what is safe and nourishing for them. Instead, it allows the traumatized person to misinterpret their surroundings and the stimuli they receive from them.[24] Chronically traumatized persons no longer have a baseline state of calm and comfort; instead, they are "continually hypervigilant, anxious, and agitated."[25]

The third category of trauma is known as vicarious trauma. It is unique in that it is not the individual's traumatic experience that is the cause but instead the second-hand attachment of one person to someone else's lived trauma. People are wonderful at empathizing with another person's hurts; however, the person who does empathize risks vicarious trauma, which can sometimes lead to them assimilating that person's trauma as their own. Clergy are in the category of caregivers who can be affected by vicarious trauma, for it "can affect first responders and people in other helping professions, but it can also affect any compassionate person who doesn't shy away from the suffering of others."[26] Due to the nature of the profession, as one where we care for congregants' spiritual, emotional, and even physical needs, clergy may be prone to vicarious trauma. In addition, clergy will undoubtedly experience moments where they are personally experiencing a traumatic event, which, when combined with secondary trauma, compounds the effects of personal trauma they have experienced. In her work *Trauma and Pastoral Care*, Carla Grosch-Miller states that clergy and first responders are "susceptible to delayed trauma reactions and to becoming vicariously or secondarily traumatized."[27] That secondary trauma experienced by clergy can accumulate on the care giver and manifest itself in a wide variety of symptoms later. Because of the compounding nature of direct and indirect trauma on clergy, there needs to be special attention paid to the effects of these phenomena on the lives of the pastors, as they are highly susceptible to burnout, just like others in caring professions.[28]

---

24. Van der Kolk, *Body Keeps*, 99.
25. Herman, *Trauma and Recovery*, 86.
26. Conti, *Trauma*, 21.
27. Grosch-Miller, *Trauma and Pastoral Care*, 54.
28. Reimer, "Pastoral Well-Being," 2. The study finds that on a scale of 1–10 where 10 indicates the most stress, 43.8 percent of pastors relate to the researchers that they were currently at a stress level of 7 or higher. In the DSM-5 as well as other literature such as Van der Kolk's *The Body Keeps the Score*, stress and trauma are often associated one with the other.

The fourth category of trauma is post-trauma syndromes. People immediately think of PTSD (post-traumatic stress disorder) when they hear the word trauma and post-trauma syndromes. While it is true that PTSD can be caused by trauma, it is not the only outcome for a person experiencing trauma. Post-trauma syndromes are "the array of problems that affect a person's life in a negative way after trauma occurs."[29] Post-trauma syndrome's effects make the sufferer feel out of control. Van der Kolk states, "These posttraumatic reactions feel incomprehensible and overwhelming. Feeling out of control, survivors of trauma often begin to fear that they are damaged to the core and beyond redemption."[30] In order to protect themselves, the person who is experiencing post-traumatic syndrome will go to excessive lengths to ward off intrusive symptoms. Judith Herman posits that these efforts to ward off the symptoms are "self-protective in intent, further aggravates the post-traumatic syndrome, for the attempt to avoid reliving the trauma too often results in a narrowing of consciousness, a withdrawal from engagement with others, and an impoverished life."[31] The 5th edition of the *Diagnostic and Statistics Manual of Mental Disorders* says that while in some cases symptoms of trauma can be understood within fear and anxiety based context they often, "exhibit a phenotype in which, rather than anxiety or fear-based symptoms, the most prominent clinical characteristics are anhedonic and dysphoric symptoms, externalizing angry and aggressive symptoms, or dissociative symptoms."[32] This large and varied list of symptoms reveals that the effects of someone suffering from post-trauma syndrome can be wide-ranging and affect many areas of their lives.

Clergy sometimes have the misconception that because of their calling into ministry by God, the effects of trauma on the body and the central nervous systems will not happen to them. Unfortunately, this is not the case, as clergy are not some sort of superhuman entity who are not affected by trauma; instead, they are equally susceptible to its effects. When the additional complication of vicarious trauma is added to the clergy's experience, it compounds the effects. Justine Allain-Chapman, a priest within the

29. Conti, *Trauma*, 21. Conti explains that there are seven criteria which constitute post–trauma syndrome. Exposure, re–experience, hypervigilance, increased baseline anxiety, decreased baseline mood, inadequate sleep, and behavior change (*Trauma*, 21–25).

30. Van der Kolk, *Body Keeps*, 2.

31. Herman, *Trauma and Recovery*, 42.

32. American Psychiatric Association and American Psychiatric Association, eds., *Diagnostic and Statistical Manual of Mental Disorders*, 265.

Anglican church, describes this vicarious suffering in this anecdote, "As a new pastor I experienced being overwhelmed by witnessing such suffering, and also found that suffering resonating with me so that I felt pain that somehow was—and yet wasn't—mine."[33] In *Trauma and Pastoral Care*, the author discusses the work of Dr. Sarah Horseman, whose work is to support people in Christian ministry. Horseman describes the human function curve (see figure 1), in which the amount of effort you put in determines the performance you are getting out. However, once a person reaches the top of that curve, the previous effort will not result in the same outcomes as people begin to function on overdraft energy.

Figure 1: Human Function Curve[34]

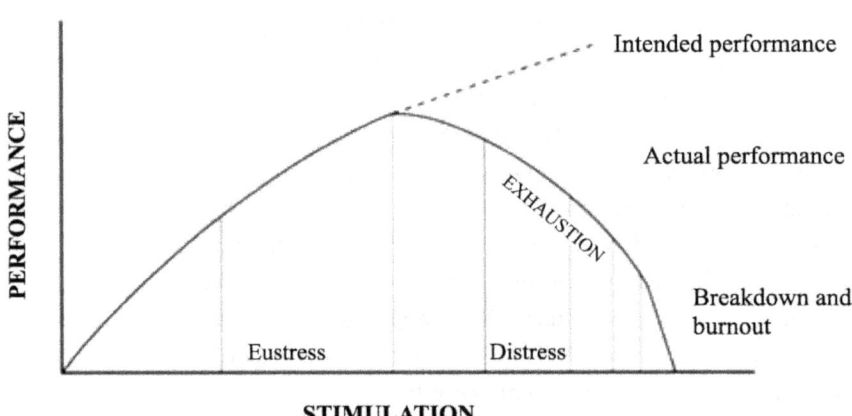

In Grosch-Miller's work, Horseman observes that many people who come for recovery at her facility in Sheldon will say they were already overstretched when an unusual time of congregational tragedy struck.[35] The effect of already being overstretched, coupled with any personal and vicarious trauma, can lead to an unhealthy pastor; spiritually, physically,

33. Allain-Chapman, *Resilient Pastors*, 4.
34. Grosch-Miller, *Trauma and Pastoral Care*, 53. The image is used with permission from Rev. Dr. Grosch-Miller and the illustrator of the image Kathy O'Laughlin. This is known as the Yerkes-Dodson Law, originally developed by psychologists Robert M. Yerkes and John Dillingham Dodson in 1908. Figure 7 is derived from the National Health Service, Scotland Deanery, www.scotlanddeanery.nhs.scot/trainee-information/thriving-in-medicine/resilience-stress-and-a-growth-mindset/, accessed 8.12.2020. The original is attributed to Dr Peter Nixon.
35. Grosch-Miller, *Trauma and Pastoral Care*, 53.

and emotionally. This exhaustion builds and causes them to appear, as Melander says, "like hosts who run around catering to the needs of their guests. They make sure everyone else is fed, even while they may themselves be hungry."[36] This lack of self-care leads to a depletion of personal resources to help others. Initially, when energy is high, the clergy can deal with a large variety of needs. However, when their energy is used up, the minor trauma, whether personal or vicarious, can cause the clergy to become overwhelmed quickly.[37] In prioritizing care for others over their own care they quickly become overwhelmed in the face of trauma when all their energy is spent.

People who have experienced trauma often tell "highly emotional stories in a highly emotional, contradictory, and fragmented manner which undermines their credibility and thereby serves the twin imperatives of truth-telling and secrecy."[38] However, it is not until the truth is told that recovery begins to manifest itself. This telling of their truth helps to reverse the core experiences of psychological trauma, which are disempowerment and disconnection from others. Recovery from trauma is based on empowering the traumatized person along with their ability to create new connections. According to Herman, recovery can "take place only within the context of relationships; it can not occur in isolation."[39] One of the conclusions from the study by Vaccarino and Gerritsen is that clergy need to ensure that they have a network established that includes people to whom they are accountable. Doing this ensures that the clergy are maintaining healthy self-care practices.[40]

Having networks of people, as well as an organized routine of self-care, will enable the clergy to begin to heal from traumatic responses. In addition, healing from trauma begins when the traumatized person can articulate their trauma. Since clergy put value on spiritual practices and often counsel people to pray and meditate to God, that should be of utmost importance as a tool for clergy when dealing with trauma. Practical

---

36. Melander, *Spiritual Leader's Guide to Self-Care*, 158.

37. Vaccarino and Gerritsen, "Exploring Clergy Self-Care." This study explores the concepts behind clergy self-care. One of the main conclusions is that often clergy do not spend adequate time and resources in caring for their own needs. It finds that many who participated in the study worked dangerously long hours and do not take the time for personal rest and rejuvenation even though they acknowledge that self-care is important.

38. Herman, *Trauma and Recovery*, 1.

39. Herman, *Trauma and Recovery*, 133.

40. Vaccarino and Gerritsen, "Exploring Clergy Self-Care," 78.

theologian John Swinton in discussing Walter Brueggemann's work with the Psalms, declares that "some of the psalms, particularly the lament psalms, are intended to function therapeutically in enabling people who have experienced deep trauma, suffering, and injustice to articulate their pain and find new ways of perceiving their situation and understanding the world."[41] In speaking of depression which he states could be caused by biology, psychology or trauma, Swinton states that the experiences of his study participants reveal that "spirituality has the potential to offer meaning in the midst of meaninglessness and hope in the face of extreme hopelessness."[42] It is within relationships that healing from trauma occurs, and spiritual relationships are an avenue which must be explored in this process.[43] Theologians and neurobiologists affirm that human beings thrive in loving relationships, and when these relationships are denied or destroyed, they will then suffer.[44] Through their spirituality, clergy can build back what has been pulled down through trauma. However, the current Pentecostal theological perspective does not fully realize suffering and trauma as a time for growth.

OVERVIEW OF PENTECOSTAL THEOLOGY

In the early 1900s, when the North American Pentecostal movement started making waves across the continent and the world, they did not see themselves as a new group or revelation but rather as a restoration of the apostolic faith. Among early Pentecostals especially, there was a belief that the movement was, according to Donald Dayton, "nothing less than God's providential restoration of the apostolic faith."[45] While this was their early emphasis, their beliefs on this would change over the years, and they would find themselves incorporating the theological ideologies of other groups.

---

41. Swinton, *Finding Jesus*, 89.

42. Swinton, *Spirituality*, 131.

43. Van der Kolk, *Body Keeps*, 212. Here he lists religious communities as one of the areas of relationship where the traumatized person can find healing. Grosch-Miller, *Trauma and Pastoral Care*, 116. Shares that in ppost–traumatic growth one of the five areas which manifest growth are spiritual/existential. This lends credence to the idea that there needs to be a spiritual dimension in order to achieve healing from trauma.

44. Ison, "Embodied and Systemic," 61. This section of the book highlights the idea of relationship being the foundation to our capacity as humans. Ison also posits that coming through such tragedy and trauma leaves scars, but also can be used to build personal and community resilience.

45. Dayton, *Theological Roots*, 35.

Trauma Studies & Theological Analysis

It would not be historically unusual if Pentecostals incorporated some of Luther's ideals, such as his *theologia crucis* and his focus on lament. To this end, an exploration of examples where Pentecostals incorporate other theologies is undertaken, showing that it is not uncommon for Pentecostals to utilize the theology of others when it suits their purpose. In North America, Pentecostalism found its roots within the Wesleyan-Holiness movement, through which much of the existing Pentecostal theology is derived from adaptations from that stream of thinking. The Wesleyan mindset brought the underlying Arminian and Methodist perfectionist motifs, adding "fuel to the optimistic expansionism of the era."[46]

Pentecostals did not just incorporate the theology of the Wesleyan-Holiness traditions; Pentecostals have a long history of incorporating the theological ideals of others while implementing their unique slant to those theological concepts. Pentecostals do this to assert their orthodox belief and align themselves historically to those belief systems, which would be considered congruent with an orthodox Christian position. Dayton gives several examples of the Pentecostals appropriating theological concepts. One prime example given is that of the Pentecostal Fellowship of North America (PFNA) in 1948, incorporating into their "Statement of Truth" large parts from the "Statement of Faith" of the National Association of Evangelicals (NAE), which was promulgated five years earlier. Dayton also quotes the Pentecostal Fellowship of North America's doctrinal statement on pages 19–21 of his book. There is reference made to the restoration of the doctrine of justification by faith through Luther, the restoration of the gospel of sanctification by faith through the Wesleys, and the restoration of divine healing through various others. These references in a decidedly Pentecostal doctrinal statement reveal they utilized and modified other classical Christian traditions when it suited them.[47]

Pentecostals also draw upon the theology of subsequence from the Roman and Anglo-Catholic distinction of Spirit and water baptism. In subsequence, the Roman and Anglo-Catholics believe that the Spirit is imparted as a subsequent event to water baptism. Pentecostals use the same logic but apply it not to water baptism and Spirit baptism but to salvation and Spirit baptism. It can also be demonstrated that Pentecostals undertake theological incorporation again if you examine the connection between the Puritan teaching on the Spirit and the link between how Puritans and

---

46. Dayton, *Theological Roots*, 64.
47. Dayton, *Theological Roots*, 17–21.

Pentecostals both emphasized eschatology and latter-day glory. German Pietism's theology of being able to overcome is used by Pentecostals as well. It is clear that Pentecostals voraciously incorporated the theology of others so that it would place them in a position of theological orthodoxy.[48] This incorporation would mean that the majority of Pentecostals in North America would align theologically with the broader Evangelical community, save for the contemporary usage of the gifts of the Spirit, with which they would differ mainly from those who held to a Reformed theological viewpoint. Usage of theologies from other Christian communities allowed the Pentecostals to quite easily align themselves with the National Association of Evangelicals in 1952 and thus be seen as participating in the broader Evangelical conversation.

Those outside the Pentecostal circle have mistakenly associated Pentecostal theology with all things pneumatological.[49] However, if adequately examined, one would see that Pentecostalism is Christocentric in nature. It is Jesus who is the center of the theology of Pentecostals. The specific focus of Pentecostal theology will be through the Pentecostal Assemblies of Canada (PAOC) lens since the people in the phenomenological interviews are all clergy with the PAOC and its sister organization in Newfoundland and Labrador, the Pentecostal Assemblies of Newfoundland and Labrador (PAONL). Four key Christocentric doctrinal starting points within these two groups shape their theological responses to situations. These fundamental elements paint a fourfold view of Jesus as savior, healer, baptizer in the Holy Spirit, and soon coming King. These four items would colloquially be known as the "full gospel." Dayton declares these are the "four Christological themes defining the basic *gestalt* of Pentecostal thought and *ethos*."[50] This work contends that a sense of triumphalism is fostered within this

---

48. Dayton, *Theological Roots*, 35–38. Dayton discusses the borrowing of theological concepts from the three streams of Anglo/Roman Catholicism, Puritanism, and German Pietism in fuller detail in these pages.

49. Dayton, *Theological Roots*, 16. Dayton advances that those who examine Pentecostal Theology often focus on pneumatological issues, especially glossolalia, which fails to see the more complex gestalt in Pentecostal theology, especially among the early Pentecostals.

50. Dayton, *Theological Roots*, 173. The four-fold theological emphasis comes from the more baptistic branch of Pentecostalism. The other branch, which is more holiness oriented, would incorporate a fifth item of theological purpose and see Jesus as sanctifier (entire) and the other four items previously listed. The holiness branch believes in a moment of entire sanctification. The baptistic branches regard sanctification as a process (progressive) rather than a distinct moment.

full gospel approach and is inherent in Pentecostal circles, the PAOC and PAONL included.

Pentecostals have seen themselves in the past and continue to some extent today as a restoration movement. That focus brings the idea of being victorious in all situations because they are on a mission from God. Specifically, Pentecostals hold a view in regard to the gifts of the Holy Spirit, which brings with it the concept of the restoration of the enduement of power as first experienced in the upper room in Acts 2. Additionally, the eschatological concept of Jesus as soon coming King harnesses the triumphalist mindset. It allows the Pentecostals to believe that we are agents in ushering in the new eschatological age. The two preceding items and equating blessings in one's life to the approval of God lead to theology that is unprepared when a trauma befalls believers who identify as Pentecostals.

Pentecostal Theology: Power Motifs in Holy Spirit Baptism

For Pentecostals, the purpose of Spirit baptism is not for receiving glossolalia or any other gift but for the enduement of power to complete the Great Commission. While all adherents understood this in the movement's early years, it has become less clear in recent years, and the emphasis has shifted mainly to the utilization of the sign gifts for personal power. Even though the modern understanding has changed, we can see that the early Pentecostals continued the tradition of drawing from the theology of other streams of Christianity by appropriating the theological concept of enduement of power for mission from the late nineteenth-century revivalists such as Finney, Moody, and later Torrey. Power enduement is now firmly entrenched in the Pentecostal ethos, and it was from this tradition that the "Pentecostal baptism of the Holy Ghost" came to prominence.[51] This baptism for the revivalists was for an enduement of power for witness without the added spiritual gifts which Pentecostals believe. Additionally, the concept that the Pentecostal "tarry and wait" for the enduement of power from above signified an eschatological breaking in of the Spirit to bring about perfection in the believer.[52]

---

51. Dayton, *Theological Roots*, 102. This section uses much common Pentecostal rhetoric, but it should be noted while the wording is similar the connection to spiritual gifts as Pentecostals view them is not present in the revivalist mindset.

52. Dayton, *Theological Roots*, 152.

According to Steven Land, this is the same conceptual framework Pentecostals hold. His treatises on the enduement of power and an eschatological connection among Pentecostals reveal a strong belief amongst them that they were ushering in the last days in fulfillment of Joel 2:28.[53] The clinging to the power narrative leads to a sense of Christian triumphalism, which Courey says represents the "immediate embrace of the entire victory of the resurrected Christ with little recognition of the world of tensions and ambiguities in which the church is called to offer her witness."[54] Pentecostals then focus on the here and now regarding victory without regard to our earthly existence's sin, suffering, and sorrow. While Pentecostals state that they believe in an already but not yet state, their practices lean heavily on seeking blessing now and do not emphasize the not yet state.

Additionally, Pentecostals believe divine healing and miracles are evidence of the "presence of divine power."[55] These moments of divine healing to Pentecostals emphasizes the believer's victory through Christ over the powers and forces of evil encroaching on human life.[56] According to Veli-Matti Kärkkäinen, Pentecostal/charismatic Christianity reintroduced to Christian spirituality the "ideal of victorious Christian living, an extensive faith expectation, and emphasis on spiritual power to overcome problems in one's life."[57] Pentecostals believed and still widely believe that it is not God's will for them to experience prolonged suffering, so they hold to an attitude of overcoming. This attitude is "characteristic to Pentecostal and charismatic preaching. Often there is a heightened expectation of divine intervention, even in situations that seem impossible."[58] The power motif can be overstated to include the idea that the Christian is to be the victor in every area of their life and that no harm will befall them. Stephen Land posits that the task then of Pentecostals is to integrate the language of righteousness, love, and power in an apocalyptic desire for spiritual transformation, which informs their spirituality.[59] Thus, Pentecostals holding to this belief will be disappointed when one of the chains of righteousness, love, or power is broken; it will affect the spiritual practices of the Pentecostal

---

53. Land, *Pentecostal Spirituality*, 53–54.
54. Courey, *What Has Wittenberg*, 7.
55. Dayton, *Theological Roots*, 115.
56. Dayton, *Theological Roots*, 116.
57. Kärkkäinen, "Theology of the Cross," 150.
58. Kärkkäinen, "Theology of the Cross," 150.
59. Land, *Pentecostal Spirituality*, 11–12.

clergy member. Lloyd-Jones writes that people who are baptized in the Holy Spirit have "a sense of the glory of God, an unusual sense of the presence of God."[60] In the case of pastors going through prolonged trauma, they may begin to wonder about the love of God, the enduement of power, or even their salvation when the problem persists. If, during these traumatic times, they no longer sense that the presence of the glory of God, as Lloyd-Jones suggests is part of the baptism in the Holy Spirit, they may begin to doubt their relationship with Christ and it can affect their spiritual praxis.[61]

Pentecostals have also developed and adhered to power evangelism, which has a power-centric theology within its conceptual framework. Power evangelism would declare that the gifts, especially healing, tongues, prophecy, and the other visible gifts, are there to accentuate and validate the message they are spreading. They draw parallels between their giftings legitimizing their message and the gifts of the Holy Spirit giving credence to the early church's message. Early Pentecostals especially focused on the gifts in operation to highlight that their movement was from God. In early issues of *The Apostolic Faith*, the newsletter that originated from the Azusa Street Mission from 1906–1908, relay many accounts of miracles occurring, and those reports were used to validate the idea that power had returned to the church like it was at "The Old–Time Pentecost."[62] This conceptual framework stems from a combination of the adoption by Pentecostals of the Fundamentalist position on the infallibility of Scripture and the ideal of a Luke/Acts restoration of the power seen in the New Testament church in the modern Pentecostal movement.

Pentecostals agreed with Fundamentalists on inerrancy but also valued experience which was considered a theologically liberal position.[63] Assemblies of God (AG) scholars William and Robert Menzies describe this tension by pointing out that Pentecostals tend to emphasize experience

---

60. Lloyd-Jones, *Joy Unspeakable*, 85.

61. Lloyd-Jones, *Joy Unspeakable*, 157. It is at this point where Lloyd-Jones suggests that the baptism in the Holy Spirit is the "highest form of assurance of salvation that anybody can ever receive, and that with this assurance comes the power." The author here is seen using a common Pentecostal theological position that marries the baptism in the Holy Spirit with proof of salvation and power for service.

62. "The Old–Time Pentecost," 1. Many more examples from this newsletter series can be seen by visiting https://www.azusabooks.org/papers.shtml. This is not limited to just the papers out of Azusa, it can be seen in many of the newsletters from various sources in the Pentecostal movement.

63. Torr, *A Dramatic*, 101–02.

coupled with their position on Biblical inerrancy, which "had led Pentecostals to develop their own theology of power evangelism."[64] Pentecostals derive their power evangelism pattern from the Lukan body of work. The Menzies duo are quick to point out that Luke was aware of the potential abuses of placing too much emphasis on the miraculous. According to the two Menzies, Luke's concern was that we must be aware of the benefits of proper alignment with the enduement of power from the Holy Spirit and recognize and understand the dangers of being improperly situated. The Menzies duo warn that Pentecostals who utilize power evangelism through signs and wonders must also be aware of the trials and tribulations inherent in life to avoid "the dangers of triumphalism inherent in signs and wonders."[65] In other words, a movement that focuses on signs and wonders must not solely emphasize those aspects, especially when confronted with troubles in life that remain unresolved despite the numerous prayers offered. Pentecostals, however, have had problems avoiding the dangers of triumphalism. In *Pentecostal Experience,* Peter Neumann says that Pentecostals should have "considerable pause in their popular, and sometimes naïve, appeals to experience of the Spirit as justification for belief and practice. The history of Pentecostalism is tainted with charges (and evidence) of triumphalism, elitism, and schism (often within its own ranks)."[66] Early PAOC General Superintendent George Chambers, while ministering in Milles Roches, Ontario, described his meetings as a repetition of the book of Acts and stated that "[A]s far as I know, there was not one prayer that we offered to God that was not answered."[67] Neumann believes that the early expression of the Canadian Pentecostal movement continues discussing triumphalism evident in Pentecostal circles by linking their triumphalistic and otherworldly spirituality to an elitist attitude that detaches the process of sanctification as demonstrated in love from the Spirit's work.[68] For Pentecostals, power evangelism leads the believer to tarry and wait for the inbreaking of power through the Holy Spirit, by which a Christian perfection

---

64. Menzies and Menzies, *Spirit and Power,* 152.

65. Menzies and Menzies, *Spirit and Power,* 153–54. The authors believe that a misdirected focus solely on the miraculous with no balance with the realities of a life which has suffering will lead to an unrealistic state of triumphalism.

66. Neumann, *Pentecostal Experience,* 15. The author also shares how triumphalism in Pentecostal circles has allowed them to embrace an elitist attitude when it comes to ecumenical cooperation (p. 139).

67. Miller, *Canadian Pentecostals,* 58–59.

68. Neumann, *Pentecostal Experience,* 170.

can be realized.⁶⁹ However, when this power evangelism motif is misused, it can lead to disappointment for the believer.

Revivalist Charles Finney, whom early Pentecostals styled much of their theology and praxis after, equated that the failure to get God's blessing, especially concerning revival, was due to human failure.⁷⁰ Lloyd-Jones continues that thought and relates failure to the individual's sinfulness and demonic attack.⁷¹ This mindset proposes that humanity is not meant to be miserable, and if you are; it is considered a failure, which goes against the ideals of God for us.⁷²

The power narrative in place caused Pentecostals to view opposition to their mission as demonic in nature and contrary to the desires of God. Pentecostals who were living their life in the Spirit were "to live in the kingdom. Where the Spirit was present in eschatological power, there was the church of Pentecost."⁷³ It is important to note that the enduement of power and the eschatological kingdom being immanent are linked in Pentecostal theology. It provides the eschatological framework of the Pentecostal, which drives a sense of triumphalism along with the power narrative.

Pentecostal Theology: Soon Coming King

Pentecostals have always believed in the imminent return of Christ. This belief also leads them to a sense of triumphalism in their spirituality and how they face everyday situations. In movements like Pentecostalism, pneumatological and eschatological expectations are linked. According to Dayton, people with the Spirit "seem to long most ardently for a return of Christ and a corresponding cosmic transformation of this world order."⁷⁴ Robert Mapes Anderson, whose work *Vision of the Disinherited* documents the origins and early years of the American Pentecostal movement, says

---

69. Dayton, *Theological Roots*, 152. Dayton also goes into further detail about the ideals of "Christian Perfectionism" on pages 65–68 of his work. While this idea tends to be more Holiness Pentecostal in nature, there are still trappings of it in the more baptistic Pentecostal denominations of which the PAOC is a part.

70. Dayton, *Theological Roots*, 122. According to Dayton the emphasis on revivalism in Pentecostal precedents believed that it ushers in a new era of God's special blessings (p. 153).

71. Lloyd-Jones, *Joy Unspeakable*, 215, 219, 239.

72. Lloyd-Jones, *Joy Unspeakable*, 102.

73. Land, *Pentecostal Spirituality*, 56.

74. Dayton, *Theological Roots*, 144.

that the central theme of the early Pentecostal movement was pinpointed as "Jesus is coming soon."[75] It has often been stated that Pentecostals were known to be Holy Spirit centric and focused on gifts, especially visible gifts such as healing and glossolalia. However, Anderson shares that while those were important events, they were subordinate elements in "what was first and foremost a millenarian movement."

The imminent return of Christ for Pentecostals was and remains a part of a larger conceptual framework that unified past, present, and future. To Pentecostals, the world was and remains in a mode of degradation due to the effects of sin, they believe their movement is a culmination of history, and they are the last force before Jesus returns and set up His earthly kingdom. Pentecostals, especially the founders, viewed their movement as an act of God that no force could stand against.[76] They hold to an ideal which believes this movement is exceptional and restoration of the church in the book of Acts; this view was especially strong in the early years of the movement; however, there remains some lingering theological predisposition to this ideal. Stephen Land links the Pentecostal eschatological idea to that of Karl Barth who believed prayer was an eschatological cry that combined the name of God, his will, and his reign in reality for the here and now.[77] Therefore, Pentecostals are not praying by their own power but by the unction and power of the person, will, and reign of God in these last days. In Land's work, he reveals the Pentecostal mindset of one that is otherworldly and focused on showing Pentecostals how to live in the last days. Even in the face of demonic or religious opposition and hindrances, Pentecostals believe nothing can stop God's plan from being fulfilled. The experience of Spirit baptism equips them to do spiritual battle, and they would tear down spiritual strongholds to aid them in reaching the lost.[78] If any victory is not realized, the failure is placed squarely on the believer's efforts or perhaps demonic influence. Combining the narrative of victory, the Pentecostal motif of soon coming King, and the idea that because they were living in the eschatological age of Christ's return causes the Pentecostals to

---

75. Anderson, *Vision*, 79.

76. Courey, *What Has Wittenberg*, 26. Courey posits that idea that God had ordained the Pentecostal movement into existence was a key factor in what he refers to as Pentecostal exceptionalism. With Pentecostal exceptionalism, they viewed this as a movement from God and no one else, therefore no force whether it be spiritual or natural could stand against it.

77. Land, *Pentecostal Spirituality*, 25.

78. Land, *Pentecostal Spirituality*, 84.

believe that God then would give them victory, which, in turn, leads them to have a heightened sense of triumphalism. To live in the Spirit was akin to living in the Kingdom.[79]

The last days motif was and still is a significant ideal in Pentecostal circles. Pentecostals view the twentieth-century outpouring of the Spirit at Azusa and other places as a sign that God has broken in and is beginning to fulfill the prophecy of Joel 2:28. Through the fulfillment of that prophetic promise, Pentecostals believe themselves to be the group through whom the world will be evangelized by their empowering through the Spirit. The demonic powers and principalities will be thwarted, and Pentecostals can live "in an apocalyptic existence made existentially palpable by the presence, manifestations and power of the Holy Spirit."[80] The gifts of the Spirit now being given to these Pentecostals, especially in the early years, signified that they were part of the end-time will of God, against which nothing would stand. This unique sense of calling and purpose added to the triumphalistic rhetoric, allowing it to take a firm hold.[81]

Pentecostal Theology: Triumphalism and Suffering

As it is with any movement that believes they are at the centre of God's will and who hold to such a deep feeling of triumph, Pentecostals struggle to understand their suffering theologically. PAOC theologian David Courey suggests that Pentecostals experience a tension between the "promise of power, and the frustration of disappointed experience."[82] Courey's premise is that because this promise ends in disappointment, there is a disillusionment that is painful on a personal level. In contrast, on the institutional level, the continued rhetoric of the promise of power is viewed through institutional success rather than individual embitterment. Pentecostals believe they are to live the victorious Christian life, even when reality suggests

---

79. Land, *Pentecostal Spirituality*, 56–57. Land shows in this section of his work that to the Pentecostal, to be Spirit filled brought on a sense of empowerment that would enable them to help usher in the eschatological age. Page 66 of Land's work reveal the idea that Pentecostals believed that the cross represented a daily victory.

80. Land, *Pentecostal Spirituality*, 58.

81. Courey, *What Has Wittenberg*, 73. For Courey the Pentecostal has a sense of immediacy in which they will experience God through the Spirit which is also marked by an "acute eschatological expectancy."

82. Courey, *What Has Wittenberg*, 2.

that life is not as good as anticipated.[83] They typically reject anything that may conflict with their sense of triumph; some blame the negative experiences on unconfessed sin or spiritual forces rising against them. The theology of Pentecostal believers is that they will always have victory.

However, when victory does not occur, they are left wondering what went wrong, which reveals an inadequacy in the theological lens through which Pentecostals interpret life events, especially negative ones. When the realities of life are not in line with the sense of triumph that is endemic in Pentecostal circles, they disregard it and move away from the trauma without dealing entirely with it. When death is not defeated, or sickness is not overcome, the reaction of Pentecostals is to call upon the eventual victory they see in the cross and resurrection; all the while, they ignore their current pains and sufferings. They utilize the imagery of the cross without looking at the suffering of Christ upon it as something that we, too, can learn from. Instead, Pentecostals only want the experience of the blessings of God. Dealing with the suffering would make them uncomfortable because it clashes with their theology of triumph.

Lloyd-Jones' statement embodies what Pentecostals expected in their experience with baptism in the Holy Spirit and the rest of life. For Pentecostals, "another pronounced characteristic that always accompanies it is an assurance of the love of God to us in Jesus Christ."[84] While it is true that God's love is displayed to us, the Pentecostal experience has always sought those Hallelujah moments which underscore the inherent triumphalism which "has had a long and deep history in the Pentecostal ethos, and profound antecedents in American religious history."[85] Suffering was never the focus of Pentecostals; instead, they viewed suffering and persecution as an existential link to the early church and its suffering. Linking their experience with the early church brought legitimacy to their cause and helped them identify with the inaugural Holy Spirit event in the upper room. Suffering was endured but never focused on; you did not analyze what you were going through in suffering. Instead, you prayed it away, and

---

83. Courey, *What Has Wittenberg*, 3. The author also highlights the usage of terms such as "the power of Spirit–filled living" as well as the push of Pentecostal success as the fastest growing movement in the world as an indication of the idea that triumph is inevitable.

84. Lloyd-Jones, *Joy Unspeakable*, 89.

85. Courey, *What Has Wittenberg*, 71. Courey also covers the idea that Pentecostal triumphalism is a species of the larger genus of triumphalism in evangelical circles on page 25 of his work.

if it remained, you purposed in your heart to still live a joy-filled life, even if that was impossible. However, when joy was no longer an option because the circumstances of life became unbearable, Pentecostal theology does not offer an avenue to consider your pain. Perhaps the solution to this is not complex, and Pentecostals need to add another aspect to their theology. Courey suggests this can be found in the theology of the cross of Martin Luther, which we will now examine.[86]

LUTHER'S THEOLOGY OF THE CROSS AS A PENTECOSTAL CONVERSATION PARTNER

As noted above, Pentecostals have long had problems dealing with the negative side of the Christian life. When they face disappointment, tragedy strikes, or prayers go unanswered, it has left many Pentecostals with few options. They are left "either to deny experiences that seem to shatter one's faith, to blame oneself or other persons involved for the lack of faith, or to give up one's faith."[87] There is a need in Pentecostal circles to have a method to confront situations that prove difficult or tiresome. The previous sections of this chapter highlight the lack of such a method or such a theology within existing Pentecostal theology and praxis.

However, there is no need for Pentecostals to invent something entirely new to aid them when dealing with trauma and suffering in their midst. Luther's theology of the cross is an existing theology that will allow Pentecostals to consider their suffering as something that can shape them spiritually. Pamela Engelbert suggests that Luther's theology of the cross "challenges Pentecostals to consider life's dark side rather than only the sentimentality of God's love."[88] Luther believed that life's dark side helped to reveal God to us through suffering and the cross. Luther's words and teachings are rife with treasure for Pentecostal believers, which is why serious consideration should be given to include his thoughts alongside Pentecostal theology.

---

86. Courey, *What Has Wittenberg*, Courey's book deals extensively with Luther's theology of the cross as a potential conversation partner for existing Pentecostal theology. Courey's interaction with Lutheran theology will be highlighted in the next section in further detail as he endeavours to provide a link between them.

87. Kärkkäinen, "Theology of the Cross," 151.

88. Engelbert, *Who Is Present*, 7.

In his work, David Courey argues that Luther is an ideal conversation partner for Pentecostals because he shares sympathies with Pentecostals who long for spiritual experience. Luther is one of the "most fertile, enigmatic and remarkably adaptable thinkers in the history of the church."[89] Courey does not see Luther's theology of the cross as an instrument to tear down Pentecostalism's existing theology; instead, he believes that there is much value in a synthesis between existing Pentecostal theology and Luther's *theologia crucis* (theology of the cross), which would provide a "constructive corrective that affirms some of the basic impulses of Pentecostalism."[90]

One of the synergies between Luther and Pentecostals is the belief in the supernatural. While Pentecostals have often blamed the Devil for any malaise that may come their way, Luther himself realized Satan's function as something that had natural world implications. In Courey's understanding of Luther, "The reality of Satan is as essential to Luther as the notions of sin and temptation or incarnation and cross. Otherwise, the whole Christian project is a matter of mere myth or imagination."[91] Courey suggests, "For Luther, what charismatics call 'spiritual warfare' was serious business."[92] On the charismata, Luther was less convinced but open to them; Courey writes, "He does not forbid the exercise of charismata, nor does he claim that they are no longer possible. Rather he acknowledges that "now until the end of the world He gives the Holy Spirit and the gifts secretly and invisibly to his Christians, and he urges caution."[93]

Luther posits in the *Heidelberg Disputation* in thesis number twenty that "But he is worthy to be called a theologian who looks at the hidden things and "backside" of God (*posteriori Dei*) [Exodus 33:23] as being seen through sufferings and the cross."[94] Luther's theology of the cross holds that God is not only revealed in the moments of glory but also in the moments of suffering. It allows the relationship between God and humanity

---

89. Courey, *What Has Wittenberg*, 2.

90. Courey, *What Has Wittenberg*, 115. Courey in the pages following points out that Luther himself had a worldview and belief system which allowed for the operation of the supernatural, this would be considered a natural connection point with Pentecostals.

91. Courey, *What Has Wittenberg*, 117.

92. Courey, *What Has* Wittenberg, 118.

93. Courey, *What Has Wittenberg*, 120.

94. Luther, "Heidelberg Disputation (1518)."

to be "held in tension in a world filled with sin and suffering."[95] However, Pentecostal circles tend to minimize the sufferings with which people are afflicted; suffering is not often viewed as a possible avenue for spiritual growth. Pentecostals attribute suffering to either the lack of God's blessings or demonic influence; this indicates that Pentecostals hold to what Luther would call a theology of glory and hold an idea that we have something to offer God. Luther's position on suffering was entirely different in that he believed we offer nothing of value.

Luther's theology of the cross declares that the believer brings nothing of value to the relationship with God. Everything we have in our relationship with God is imparted through His grace. In thesis twenty-one, Luther declares that "a theology of glory calls evil good and good evil. A theology of the cross calls the thing what it actually is."[96] Courey, on this point, warns that some have used it to paint the sufferer in the role of the victim. We should not take on the victim role; instead, we should understand that "the fundamental issue with the human condition is called sin. Without an acknowledgement of this there can be no progress."[97] Luther believed that sinful humans brought nothing to their relationship with God, and everything we received was due to God's nature and doing. When humans craft their own narrative there is a tendency to always see themselves as the one who is the hero of the story. This mindset leads to us describing situations where we present ourselves in the best light possible. We are the undeserved victims when something goes wrong and the heroes when something goes well. This self-confidence needs to be challenged, and Kärkkäinen believes that happens through a realized theology of the cross. "In this way, the theology of the cross destroys man's self-confidence and at the same time elevates God. God is free and sovereign to do whatever he wishes."[98]

Kärkkäinen also believes that Pentecostals who are used to the faith formulas like "name it and claim it" would be well served to ponder the ideas Luther found in thesis twenty-four of the *Heidelberg Disputation*. Luther's thesis describes the person who has been emptied through suffering as one who no longer does the works themselves but realizes "that God works and does all things in him. For this reason, whether God does works or not, it is all the same to him. He neither boasts if he does good works, nor is he

95. Kärkkäinen, "Theology of the Cross," 153.
96. Luther, "Heidelberg Disputation (1518)."
97. Courey, *What Has Wittenberg*, 156.
98. Kärkkäinen, "Theology of the Cross," 157.

disturbed if God does not do good works through him. He knows that it is sufficient if he suffers and is brought low by the cross."[99] We can not claim victory; we are powerless to do so; it is only through God's grace that we have anything. Kärkkäinen suggests six ways in which Pentecostals are able to utilize Luther's theology of the cross which will be used as a framework for the rest of this work when considering implementing Luther's *theologia crucis* in Pentecostal theology and praxis. His six points are as follows: first, the problem of evil must be faced in all its seriousness and ugliness;[100] Second, the cross of Christ has not only salvatory but also revelational importance.[101] Third, the essence of God's love means loving something that is nonexistent, or that exists in weakness and shame, to make it something new.[102] Fourth, God assumes the final responsibility for evil and suffering in the world, and humanity must leave it with God.[103] Fifth, Christian theology about evil should be a theology of hope.[104] And sixth, we may suffer as individuals but recover in community.[105] Suppose this theology were added

---

99. Luther, "Heidelberg Disputation (1518)."

100. Kärkkäinen, "Theology of the Cross," 162. Kärkkäinen believes that much of the Pentecostal/charismatic spirituality and theology is a misguided effort to whitewash the world with a form of sentimentality in our talk about God.

101. Kärkkäinen, "Theology of the Cross," 162. The author here suggests that for Luther, revelation is the word of the cross. Everything that can be said about God or his world is mediated by the cross.

102. Kärkkäinen, "Theology of the Cross," 162. Kärkkäinen suggests that much of the love talk surrounding God in Pentecostal circles is vague. Pentecostals have tended to focus on the grace of God and not paid much attention to this category of love, but if they did give it focus and combined it with the biblical, especially Old Testament view of God's love, it might help Pentecostals to have something worthwhile to say about God's *agape* love.

103. Kärkkäinen, "Theology of the Cross," 162. For Luther evil and suffering are God's responsibility, and the cross reveals that God find the solution to the problem. While Pentecostals believe God has dealt with sin on the cross, in praxis they often see suffering as being related to personal sin and they look for ways to remedy the sin outside of the cross, so that they may again experience blessing.

104. Kärkkäinen, "Theology of the Cross," 162–63. Because Luther's theology of the cross takes suffering and death seriously it also takes hope seriously. However, with Pentecostal they often use the concept of faith in terms of that hope. Pentecostals need to examine that hope but in doing so move the faith from human action to something God does. In other words, Pentecostals must move from a mindset that says "If I believe enough" to one that says "I trust God."

105. Kärkkäinen, "Theology of the Cross," 163. Pentecostals must regain a sense of community of faith that was present in the early church and move away from an individualistic idea of salvation.

to the existing Pentecostal theology. In that case, it will allow them to seek still the experiences of power that have been a hallmark of the movement and see the idea of continued suffering as a place where we meet God; this would allow the person going through extended suffering not to view their position as one of spiritual failure or God-forsakenness but instead as a place to draw into the presence of God through identification with the suffering on the cross.

LOOKING FORWARD

The typically Pentecostal mindset inherent in its theology is that God has enabled them to be victorious. Pentecostals view the victory from God as an imperative to fulfill the mission to which He has called them. As we have seen in the preceding pages, the victory ideal comes from the triumphalistic attitudes that Pentecostals possess. Their belief in the soon coming King and their focus on healing, combined with their general end times affections, cause them to believe that nothing will thwart them. When problems arise, they often attribute these to a lack of personal faith, sin in their lives, or some otherworldly demonic force fighting against them. However, the reality of life does not often match the theological position that Pentecostals have. There are times and situations where the victory is not present and may never be present for the sufferer. Pentecostals who suffer trauma can not consider themselves different from the rest of society. As we have seen in the above pages, trauma is insidious. It affects a majority of Canadian Christians at one point in their lives or others, and a healthy approach to trauma for Pentecostals is necessary. Instead of simply believing that the trauma will go away, they should instead embrace the suffering, as Lutheran theology suggests, and use it as a point to further develop their spiritual praxis. The Pentecostal theology of glory should be supplemented with a theology of the cross that allows God to be revealed during those dark moments of the soul. The following two chapters of this book specifically deal with how PAOC and PAONL clergy have experienced trauma and obtained that data.

Chapter 3 of the book presents the study's research methodology, which is phenomenology. It provides a brief overview of the history of phenomenology and the phenomenological method of Max Van Manen, whose system is utilized in this project. It describes how phenomenological interviews were conducted with Pentecostal clergy from the PAOC and

PAONL. The preliminary data from those interviews is published in chart form and through brief commentary on them in the conclusion of this chapter, a fuller exploration of the phenomenon takes place in chapter 4.

In chapter 4, the interviews are analyzed, and ample quotes are utilized from the interviews to highlight the seven main essences of trauma through the participants' words. It allows the essences of trauma to be accurately reflected as they had experienced them. Crafted anecdotal narratives, which Van Manen suggests, are utilized to highlight the essence of the trauma in the minds of the readers of this work. Mention is also given about the spiritual practices which the interview subjects undertook. Any significant changes to those practices because of trauma was also noted. In addition, any theological reflection that the participants made is recorded in the later sections of this chapter.

3

Research Methodology and Design

THREE TOOLS ARE UTILIZED during this research phase. First, the study is based on practical theology, so an overview of practical theology and its importance for this research is established. Next, an explication of the concepts behind practice-led research is given to highlight its significance to this project. Phenomenology and practical theology are known to "share the importance of expression or vocalizing a concrete experience."[1] This shared importance makes phenomenology best suited as the method of understanding the experiences of the pastors interviewed for this study. We study trauma as lived experience to gain a better insight into the phenomenon. Campbell declares that scholars utilize phenomenology in the study of suffering so that "we may articulate suffering as lived, embodied experience."[2] Therefore embodied experience of trauma in the pastor's life is brought into view through phenomenology to explore it more fully by both the researcher and the research participant.

After a description of practical theology and practice-led research is established, this chapter briefly discusses the concepts behind phenomenology, its inception, and its rise to prominence under the direction of Edmund Husserl in the early twentieth century, after which an exploration of the phenomenological practices of Max Van Manen is considered. Van

---

1. Zylla, "Shades of Lament," 765.
2. Campbell, "Glory in Suffering?," 520.

Manen's approach is utilized during the qualitative research phase of this work; this requires an explanation of the philosophical assumptions within those phenomenological practices as they shape the direction of the study. Being more aware of the philosophical principles behind Van Manen's method allows us to discuss the research design which was followed in fuller complexity. During this discussion, a description of the participants with whom the research was conducted is established.

This study was conducted amongst Canadian Pentecostal clergy within the denominations of the Pentecostal Assemblies of Canada (PAOC) and the Pentecostal Assemblies of Newfoundland and Labrador (PAONL) who have experienced trauma. The details of each participant's background and the specific trauma they have experienced will be explored further in chapter 4.

PRACTICAL THEOLOGY AND PRACTICE-LED RESEARCH

Since the impetus behind this undertaking is centered around both practical theology and practice-led research; this section offers an overview of each, giving insight into shaping and contributing to the research direction.

Practical Theology

According to Osmer, practical theology focuses on answering four foundational questions; "What is going on? Why is this going on? What ought to be going on? How might we respond?"[3] The process of answering these questions is the emphasis of the four core tasks of practical theological interpretation, which together constitute its framework. As we examine each of these tasks laid out by Osmer, we will begin to understand their importance in this research.

The first task of practical theological interpretation is the descriptive-empirical task.[4] This task requires the researcher to gather the information that will help them discover patterns that appear in situations, events, or contexts. For this study, the tool utilized in the descriptive-empirical

---

3. Osmer, *Practical Theology*, 4.

4. Osmer, *Practical Theology*, 4. All four tasks mentioned in this paragraph come from this page of Osmer's monograph.

phase is phenomenology. Phenomenology allows patterns to be uncovered and for them to be explored in fuller detail. The second task is the interpretive task; this step requires the researcher to draw from arts and science theories to understand better why the patterns uncovered in the first task are occurring. Trauma studies are utilized in this second step to understand better how trauma affects individuals so that conversation points can occur. Understanding the scientific world of trauma studies allows the practical theologian to see and explain the patterns that are uncovered in step one.

The third task of practical theological interpretation calls for the researcher to utilize the normative task, which has the practical theologian using theological concepts to interpret the episodes, situations, and contexts. The practical theologian can then construct ethical norms that will guide our responses to the first two tasks. To utilize it in this study, we examine Pentecostal theology related to suffering and trauma and look for ways to enhance how Pentecostals can respond while experiencing trauma. The pragmatic task is the fourth of Osmer's tasks. This task calls for the practical theologian to develop strategies that will help influence the situations in desirable ways and allow us to enter reflective conversations. This study will allow us to look at what is valuable and not so valuable among Pentecostals as they respond to trauma; this will aid in answering the fourth question posited above, which then allows for an examination of Luther's theology of the cross to understand better why it is suggested as an additive to existing Pentecostal theology. Tasks one and two are primarily accomplished in chapter four of this work, and tasks three and four are accomplished primarily in chapter 5.

Practice-led Research

Pete Ward defines practical theology as "any way of thinking that takes both practice and theology seriously."[5] He declares that his description is less of a definition and more of a "decision to include within the accepted academic work in practical theology a whole range of material that might not normally be seen as belonging to the discipline."[6] His purpose in doing this is to help reverse a trend in practical theology that limits itself to those who have membership in the academic guild. Ward desires practical theology not to be solely academic but to be utilized by anyone. The ideas behind

---

5. Ward, *Introducing Practical Theology*, 5.
6. Ward, *Introducing Practical Theology*, 5.

practice-led research fit Ward's desire to transform practical theology from solely academic to incorporating the practice and practitioners together with the academics.

According to Carole Gray, practice-led research is to be initiated in the practice of the researcher. She writes that it is "initiated in practice, where questions, problems, challenges are identified and formed by the needs of practice and practitioners; and secondly, that the research strategy is carried out through practice, using predominantly methodologies and specific methods familiar to us as practitioners."[7] In this research, my trauma is brought to the forefront so that I can utilize it to better understand clergy trauma and our responses to it. Candy shares that practice-led research (PLR) differs from practice-based research (PBR) in that the latter focuses on the nature of practice, and the former gains new knowledge through practice.[8] PLR gains new knowledge by examining the practice and seeking to understand its nature, while PBR gains new knowledge from doing the practice. To further this idea, Neil Ferguson offers two helpful characteristics of PLR in his Ph.D. thesis; first, he states that the research is "investigating a problem that has arisen from within practice or as a part of an individual's practice and would not be seen outside of that practice."[9] Secondly, he says it is essential to realize that "the problem is researched within the practice and using the methods and tools of the practice."[10] So the practical theologian using PLR would find their research from their practice and use the tools found within their own area of expertise to draw knowledge out of practice.

In practice-led research, the subject of study is obtained from the researcher's practices. So then, the choice to look at trauma and how it affects the spirituality of Pentecostal clergy rises out of my own practice. I have experienced traumas in my life to varying degrees, both as a clergy member and while not a clergy member. My earliest recollection of trauma arose out of the separation and divorce of my parents when I was a child; however, that is not the trauma that spurred me to consider this project. The traumatic event that caused me to consider this study was the death of my son Dawson at the age of 4 months in 1999. When confronted with the experience, I was unsure how to act and what to do and struggled to understand

---

7. Gray, "Inquiring through Practice," 3.
8. Candy, *Practice Based Research*, 3.
9. Ferguson, "Practice–Led Theology," 119.
10. Ferguson, "Practice–Led Theology," 119.

why God could allow this to happen. Even though people surrounded me in support at these times, I often felt alone and abandoned. I did not find solace from any theological training I had acquired at a Pentecostal Bible College, and it did not prepare me to understand what was happening or how to experience God during trauma. I realized there was a deficit in my theology and praxis when it came to any suffering since the Pentecostalism I was taught often sought out the most triumphalist terms and declared we would have the "ultimate victory." My spiritual practices and my theological lens become the areas of practice under study as I examine the nature of suffering through trauma in the Pentecostal clergy person. Practical theology and PLR become valuable tools to examine the subject of this study; however, an additional tool is needed for this study to draw out the meaning of trauma in Clergy and its effects on their spiritual practices. The tool that was best suited for this examination is Phenomenology, and the next section of this chapter will explore its philosophy and methodology.

PHENOMENOLOGY AS A PHILOSOPHICAL AND METHODOLOGICAL TOOL

Phenomenology is known to have a strong philosophical aspect, drawing on the writing of mathematician Edmund Husserl.[11] These philosophical tendencies are emphasized by Cresswell and Poth's utilization of Stewart and Mikunas' four philosophical perspectives, which state that Phenomenology is a return to the traditional task of philosophy, a philosophy without prepositions, has an intentionality of consciousness, and refuses the subject-object dichotomy; this means that we obtain the gateway to understanding the phenomenon through the philosophy of the phenomenological question. In exploring the phenomenon, the researcher must first ask, "How do we form the question that makes the basis of our Phenomenological research?" Truls Åkerlund has provided insight into this by stating, "The foundational question asked in phenomenological inquiry is that of meaning, structure, and essence of the lived experience of this phenomenon for a person or group, and aims for a deeper and fuller understanding of what it is like for someone to experience something."[12] The aim then is to understand the meaning of an experience through the eyes of the person who experienced it, without the "theoretical overlay that might be put on it

---

11. Creswell and Poth, *Qualitative Inquiry*, 75.
12. Akerlund, *Phenomenology of Pentecostal Leadership*, 6–7.

by the researcher, and to provide a comprehensive and rich description of it."[13] This methodology will allow the research to probe deep into the lived experience of the interviewee so that a more precise picture can emerge.

In his work *Phenomenology of Practice*, Van Manen presents concepts utilized in this research. He posits that phenomenological questions may cause us to pause and reflect. Even the most ordinary experience will cause us to pause and will make us ask, what is this experience like?[14] Therefore, phenomenology and the phenomenological question are the backbones of the process.

This project will perform a phenomenological interview whose aim is to gather "prereflective experiential accounts."[15] In other words, the data gathered is the essence of the phenomenon before the participant, the researcher, or any other individual have analyzed it. In order for this to be accomplished, the phenomenological interview is utilized. The dual-pronged purpose is first so that it can be used to gather and explore "experiential narrative material that may serve as a resource for developing a richer and deeper understanding of human phenomenon."[16] Secondly, the interview may help develop a "conversational relationship with a partner (interviewee) about the meaning of an experience."[17]

However, prior to any phenomenological study there needs to be two steps undertaken, this is what is referred to in Phenomenology as the *epoché* and the reduction.[18] The *epoché* is the opening of oneself so that you can set aside presuppositions. At this point, the researcher acknowledges any biases or preexisting knowledge of the examined phenomenon; this does not mean the researcher no longer has that knowledge or bias, but that they are aware of them, and they can be bracketed out so that they do not affect the data gathered during the interviews and analysis. The reduction then flows from this process so that the researcher can view the phenomenon as it unfolds without bias. With these two items in place, the researcher can conduct the interviews, allowing thematizing and analysis.[19]

---

13. Swinton and Mowat, *Practical Theology*, 50.
14. Van Manen, *Phenomenology of Practice*, 31.
15. Van Manen, *Phenomenology of Practice*, 311.
16. Van Manen, *Researching Lived Experience*, 66.
17. Van Manen, *Researching Lived Experience*, 66.
18. Van Manen, *Phenomenology of Practice*, 216–18.
19. Van Manen, *Phenomenology of Practice*, 312.

Van Manen warns that any analysis of recollections of experiences, no matter which way the data is collected, is already a "transformation of those experiences."[20] The interview subjects will have already transformed what they experienced to see it through their own lens of perception. As the interview is conducted and later analyzed, the researchers ask themselves, "How does this speak to the phenomenon?"[21] Phenomenologists borrow the experiences of others, not just to gather data as many methods do, but so that we can "collect examples of possible human experiences to reflect on the meanings that may inhere in them."[22] The phenomenological interview does not seek the subjects' views, interpretations, or opinions about something; instead, the interview seeks to understand the phenomenon as the subjects had experienced them.

For this research, information about the lifeworld of clergy concerning trauma was uncovered using phenomenological interviews. Katarzyna Peoples describes the purpose of phenomenological research as "to generate the lifeworld experiences of a certain population."[23] Van Manen further explains the lifeworld as consisting of four existential elements for every human: lived space, lived body, lived time, and lived other.[24]

Lived Space (spatiality) is how space is felt by the person. When we think of space we often think of measurable distances, the mathematical space, or the dimensions of our dwellings. Lived space is more difficult to describe since "lived space (as lived time, body) is largely pre-verbal; we do not ordinarily reflect on it. And yet we know that the space in which we find ourselves affects the way we feel."[25] The feelings one encounters at the workplace will differ from the feelings and experiences they would have while sitting at their favourite coffee shop enjoying their morning coffee. Walking into a cathedral would induce different feelings than being in a bank, even if the two buildings are identical in size, shape, and layout, the feelings you experience in each can be different depending on your connection to them. Your home provides you with different feelings than another person's house, even if they are identical in every perceivable way; this is because your home has an underlying meaning to it, which is our

---

20. Van Manen, *Phenomenology of Practice*, 313.
21. Van Manen, *Phenomenology of Practice*, 312.
22. Van Manen, *Phenomenology of Practice*, 313.
23. Peoples, *How to Write*, 47.
24. Van Manen, *Researching Lived Experience*, 100–4.
25. Van Manen, *Researching Lived Experience*, 102.

"fundamental sense of being."[26] Lived space then deals with the measurable features of the place and how the person feels in that space.

According to Van Manen, lived body (corporeality) deals with the idea "that we are always bodily in the world."[27] When we meet another person face to face, we meet that person first through their physical body. In this meeting, the people simultaneously reveal and hide things about themselves; this is not necessarily done consciously or deliberately, but "in spite of ourselves."[28] The body then gets transformed by another person's gaze; it may lose its natural self or can be enhanced depending on the person gazing. In a critical gaze, the body becomes awkward and prone to discover flaws, while under the admiring gaze, the flaws become more hidden, and the beauty and grace shine out for the person gazing.

Lived time (temporality) is subjective as opposed to objective, or clock, time. In Greek mythology, objective time is personified in the god *Chronos*, who is responsible for this empirical idea of time and is viewed as being linear in nature. *Chronos* time is "plannable, measurable, reproducible, controllable, and predictable."[29] On the other side of the time spectrum, the Greeks also had a god responsible for the type of time, which is unstructured. The Greek god *Kairos* is responsible for time, where the idea is considered "creative and improvisational." *Kairos* time is living in the now and living in the moment and can be considered a timeless time. *Kairos* time, therefore, is the essence of lived time as understood in phenomenology.

Lived other (relationality) speaks of the lived relations with others in the "interpersonal space we share with them."[30] As we meet others, we approach them physically through eye contact, a smile, a nod of the head, or a myriad of other ways that acknowledge that they are physically present to us. Even if the initial contact with the person is done indirectly through telephone, letter, email, or any other non-physically present way, we have already formed a "physical impression of the person which later may get confirmed, or negated when we find out, to our surprise, that the person looks very different from the way we expected."[31]

26. Van Manen, *Researching Lived Experience*, 102.
27. Van Manen, *Researching Lived Experience*, 103.
28. Van Manen, *Researching Lived Experience*, 103.
29. Van Manen, "Serendipitous Insights," 678.
30. Van Manen, *Researching Lived Experience*, 104.
31. Van Manen, *Researching Lived Experience*, 105.

These four existentials form an "intricate unity which we call the lifeworld."[32] Even if we were to focus on one of the existentials, the others would also be brought to the forefront because one existential will beckon for the others to participate; that is the essence of the lifeworld. These existentials allow us to perceive meaning in all its richness in an immediate sense. Van Manen states that through these four, we can "perceive an immediate immense richness of meaning."[33] The lifeworld as perceived through the four existentials will be the framework of the phenomenology used in this study.

This study examines the lifeworld experiences of PAOC and PAONL clergy as it relate to their trauma, and it seeks to understand how this experience has shaped and continues to shape the person holistically; this is achieved using the phenomenological practices of Max Van Manen and his predecessors in the field of phenomenology. Through phenomenology, the researcher can better understand the implications of trauma on the person physically, emotionally, psychologically, and spiritually. The usage of phenomenology in this manner fits well into how Van Manen describes its purpose: "Phenomenology was not just the name of a philosophical perspective. It was also the source for questioning the meaning of life as we live it and the nature of responsibility of personal actions and decisions."[34] Phenomenology allows the researcher and the research participant to understand the lived experience as it was lived. Doing so makes us aware of how the experiences fashion our lives as they come to us. Van Manen continues that phenomenology "makes us mindful to be critical, and philosophically aware of how our lives (and our cognitive, emotional, embodied, and tacit understandings) are socially, culturally, politically, and existentially fashioned."[35]

So that the lifeworld can be adequately understood, what Van Manen refers to as thematic analysis was undertaken. This process utilizes a "recovering of the theme or themes that are embodied and dramatized in the evolving meanings and imagery of the work."[36] In theme analysis, the goal is to examine the methodological and philosophical character of the phenomenon. Finding the theme or themes is not based on a predetermined

---

32. Van Manen, *Researching Lived Experience*, 105.
33. Van Manen, *Researching Lived Experience*, 105.
34. Van Manen, *Phenomenology of Practice*, 13.
35. Van Manen, *Phenomenology of Practice*, 13.
36. Van Manen, *Researching Lived Experience*, 78.

set of rules; rather, it is a "free act of seeing meaning."[37] In phenomenology, when we seek the experience's themes, we try to understand and determine the "experiential structures that make up that experience."[38] We are trying to grasp what makes a thing what it is. For example, we could have a variety of baseball bats in front of us, all of different lengths, materials, and colours. The purpose of thematic analysis is to find the common features that make the thing what it is. This study uses thematic analysis to uncover the themes of trauma as experienced by the research participants.

Once we have found the themes, we next have to seek the meaning of those themes, the researcher is looking for the essence or *eidos* of the phenomenon, which is accomplished by writing each interview's themes as succinctly as possible in thematic formulations. The researcher has summarized in writing, repeatedly the phenomenon as described by the participants until it is as concise as possible. The selective or highlighting approach that Van Manen refers to was utilized to accomplish this.[39] We ask ourselves if any phrases stand out in this approach, and we highlight or circle the sentences or sentence fragments. Once we have these selections, we compose the summary sentences. Following that, the concise analysis from each interview is compared one to another. This will not provide an exhaustive list of the phenomenon's *eidos* since people are bound to experience things differently based on many internal and external factors. It will provide a reasonable understanding of the most basic essences of the phenomenon.[40]

DATA GATHERING

During the interviews, the seven pointers laid out by Van Manen for the interview process, which details the "Where, Who, When, Why, How, What, and Whatever" interview, are utilized.[41] Following these steps will

---

37. Van Manen, *Researching Lived Experience*, 79.
38. Van Manen, *Researching Lived Experience*, 79.
39. Van Manen, *Researching Lived Experience*, 94.
40. Van Manen, *Researching Lived Experience*, 87–88. See the section "What is a Theme" in these pages for better clarification on how themes are extracted during the analysis process. Of special importance the four items on the bottom of page 88 provide a deeper understanding of the nature of a theme.
41. Van Manen, *Phenomenology of Practice*, 315–16. Van Manen's point in using these steps is to provide an experience for the interviewee and interviewer that is relaxed and remains focused on the phenomenon and the research question, and also allows for

provide a far better chance the participants have felt comfortable sharing their stories. With participant comfort intact, the interviewer will be able to center on the topic and ask specific questions about the phenomenon; this will allow the interview to remain focused on the main question and remain unstructured in nature. The interviewee is able to move the experience naturally from their memory to their words. The utilization of unstructured phenomenological interviews allows for what Swinton and Mowat have deemed as "most likely to elicit rich data that would enable participants freely to relate their personal narratives."[42] The usage of the preceding steps allows the research to use Van Manen's phenomenological methods to study the phenomenon further.

The gathering of participants was accomplished through the usage of social media on a private unofficial Facebook group consisting of approximately 900 members who are PAOC or PAONL credential holders and clergy members. The researcher gave details about the study and asked anyone who might be interested in participating to contact him by email. Once contacted, the researcher sent the possible candidates an official Letter of Information and asked them to read it over and for them to contact him should they remain interested in participating in the research. Thirteen people asked for the Letter of Information, and all thirteen were willing to proceed with the study; however, two candidates were disqualified from participation in the study due to McMaster Research Ethics Board restrictions, which were in place to remove anyone with a pre-existing diagnosis of PTSD.

The remaining candidates were scheduled for a Zoom interview, during which they were first asked to describe their regular spiritual practices. Next, they were asked to recall a moment of trauma in their life and to describe it in as much detail as possible. The question used to ask them to share about their trauma was phrased like this, "Share with me a specific experience in which you have experienced trauma; please be as detailed as possible." As the interview proceeded, the participants may have been asked further clarification questions such as "What from that experience is vivid in your mind" or "How did you feel at the time—what was happening inside you—what were your bodily experiences, your mood, your emotions." All of the questions during this phase were in response to what was being shared by the participant and used to get further clarity on what a more natural conversation.

42. Swinton and Mowat, *Practical Theology*, 55.

they were saying. In the last phase of the initial interview, one final question was asked, "Did the trauma affect how you practice your spirituality?" This question was asked to understand better the perceived effects of trauma on the participants through their own eyes. Each initial interview ranged between 31 minutes to almost 2 hours and was recorded with permission to conduct a complete analysis after the interview had concluded.

After completing the interviews, each of them was transcribed, initially using the secure website enjoyhq.com. A manual transcription was then implemented to verify the accuracy of the software transcription. With the two phases of transcription complete, the interviews were analyzed to understand the phenomenon as described by the participant.

Each person's analyzed interview was sent to them, and a second Zoom interview was conducted if they had additional information to give after reading the summary provided to them; sending the summaries, as well as the second interviews, allowed for the research participants to act as data verification, as well as allowing them to give any further information on their experience with trauma. There were no formal questions asked during the second interview; instead, the conversation grew from the researcher's analysis. These second interviews were approximately 15 to 30 minutes each.

PARTICIPANTS

As previously discussed, participants came from two Canadian Pentecostal denominations. The Pentecostal Assemblies of Canada is present in every Canadian province and territory except Newfoundland and Labrador. The second denomination is the Pentecostal Assemblies of Newfoundland and Labrador, and as its name suggests, is active in the area where the PAOC is not. Both denominations are a part of the World Assemblies of God fellowship and share similar doctrinal stances. The PAOC and the PAONL cooperate to send missionaries overseas, so there is already an existing relationship between the clergy of the two entities.

Of the eleven participants, three females and eight males were interviewed, the two candidates disqualified due to PTSD were female. The ages of the eleven participants range from the early thirties to mid-sixties; ten participants are married, one is separated from their spouse, and all participants have children, some of whom are still at home while others have left the family home to start their own lives. Each participant has active

Research Methodology and Design

credentials with either the PAOC or the PAONL, and every participant is active in ministry except one who recently retired due to medical conditions. Each participant considers themselves to have experienced trauma of some sort. Further biographical information about each participant will be detailed in the next chapter's discussion of their experiences with trauma.

While not every region of the country participated, a significant portion was represented, including the west coast, the prairies, central Canada, Atlantic Canada, and Newfoundland. The three territories and Quebec were the only areas that did not have representation. Even with the non-participation of those areas, the variety provided in the other areas gives ample coverage. As a qualitative research method, phenomenology does not look for numerical data like quantitative research but looks for the essence of an experience. Therefore, the number of participants in a qualitative research project is far less critical than that of a quantitative one.[43]

DATA FROM INTERVIEWS

After the interviews were completed, transcription took place. The researcher then analyzed the transcribed interviews to find how the participants described their own experiences of trauma. In total, twenty-four separate essences were generated during analysis, and of those seven were chosen to be the main essences. They were chosen based on two criteria. The first was the prevalence of the essences across the interviews; if an essence appeared in more interviews, it was given more priority. Second, a higher frequency of appearance of an essence across all the interviews established greater importance than one which had rare occurrences. The seven essences chosen represent 86 percent of the total number generated across all documents. In contrast, the other seventeen essences not being highlighted represent the other 14 percent in the documents (Appendix 1 has a complete list of essences related to trauma). The chart below shows the percentage of time an essence was used and the number of documents in which essence appeared.

---

43. Webb, *Qualitative Dissertation*, 102–3. Webb suggests that there is no magic number for qualitative research projects. In a random sampling of articles in peer reviewed journals which publish qualitative studies, he found that most had between eight to twelve participants. Akerlund, *Phenomenology of Pentecostal Leadership*. In this study for his doctoral dissertation only four subjects were interviewed phenomenologically. The number of people is not as important in qualitative research as much as the scope of the data obtained from those interviews.

When Ministry Hurts

Figure 2: Essence % / Document Appearance

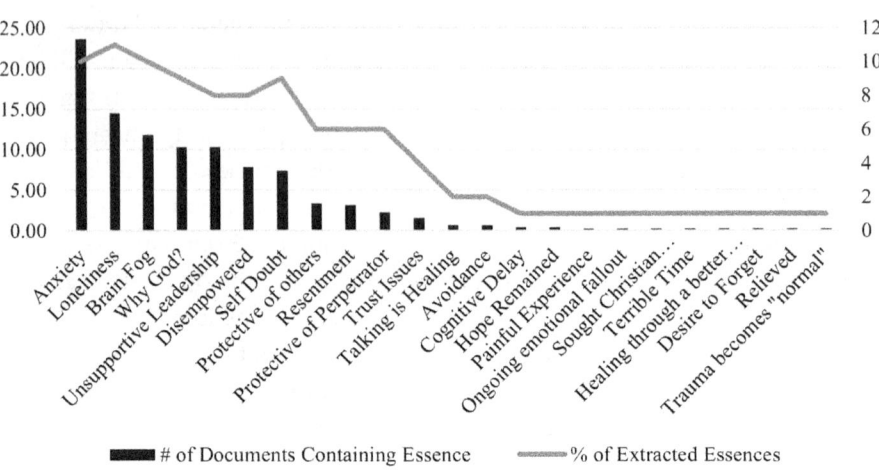

■ # of Documents Containing Essence   ── % of Extracted Essences

The list of essences used to define trauma as experienced by the participants is in the following chart; a deeper study of these will be completed in the next chapter. The numbers in the cells represent how many times the participant mentioned that particular essence. For example, we can see that Andrew's description of the way he experienced trauma was largely anxiety-based, as he had twenty-five occurrences of that particular essence within his interview.

Figure 3: Significant Essences of Trauma

	Jackie	Andrew	Danny	Connie	Paula	Kirk	Will	Jason	Shawn	Mark	Les
Anxiety	3	25	2	3	5	4	20	0	16	5	23
Loneliness	6	13	3	7	6	8	1	10	4	5	2
Brain Fog	3	4	7	1	4	11	5	2	0	15	1
Why God?	1	7	3	10	0	0	6	5	4	7	3
Unsupportive Leadership	0	6	0	0	6	7	3	3	1	2	18
Disempowered	4	3	4	0	4	4	8	0	0	1	7
Self Doubt	2	0	4	12	1	0	4	6	1	1	2

The pie chart below is presented for a straightforward visual representation of all the trauma-related essences which were retrieved during the interview and analysis portion of the research.

Research Methodology and Design

Figure 4: Essences of Trauma Graph[44]

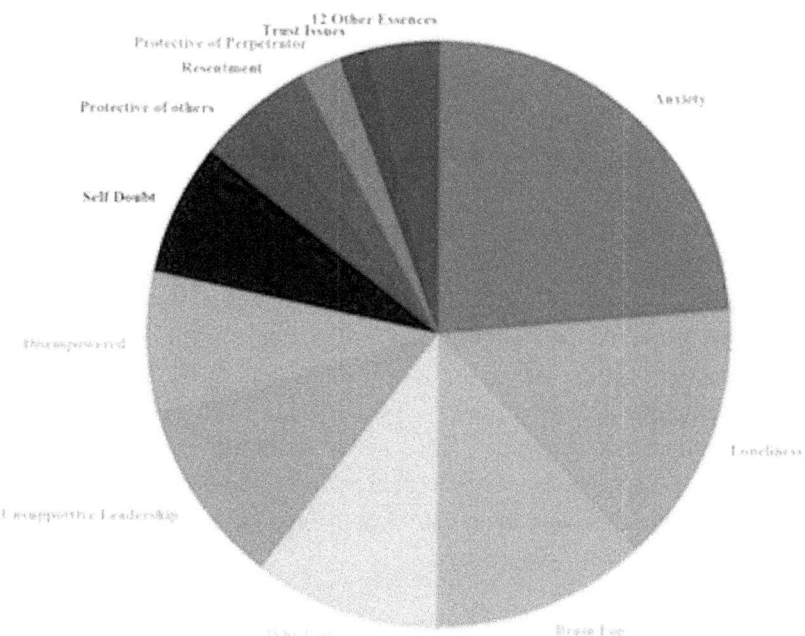

In addition to the essences of trauma noted, other notations were made that signified their regular spiritual practices. These are available in Appendix 1, along with notations that show their adapted spiritual practices; these are discussed in more detail in chapter 4 and chapter 5, and a plan is provided on how Pentecostals can better accommodate trauma theologically and in their praxis. A few mentions during the interviews were theological in nature; those are discussed in chapter 4 in part but also discussed in more detail as we explore theological implications in chapter 5.

ETHICAL CONSIDERATIONS

As with most qualitative studies, the ethical considerations for this study reflect those of most others. There are often concerns about power differentials between the researcher and the research participants in qualitative research. In this study, the researcher holds no power over the people

---

44. The label "12 Other Essences" represents a combination of essences which only appeared between one to three times each across all documents.

involved in the study, the researcher is also a credential holder in the PAOC, but he holds no position of authority over the others.

There may also arise a concern about losing privacy with the information given during the interviews. A loss of privacy or leaking of sensitive information can lead to a myriad of issues which could include but are not limited to loss of employment, being ostracized by peers, adverse reactions from those in authority over them, a loss or damaging of relationship, and a variety of other concerns too lengthy to be listed. So that concerns about a data breach may be alleviated, several steps have been undertaken. First, no data is stored on the internet but rather in portable password-protected USB drives. Second, all transcripts have been anonymized, and pseudonyms for names were used. In addition to this, no specific places are mentioned. Instead of using the community name the person resides in, the researcher has used phrases like, "A small town in Ontario" or "A larger city in British Columbia." Third, all video and audio files were deleted after manual transcription. The procedures to protect confidentiality and anonymity were approved by the McMaster Research Ethics Board.[45]

SUMMARY

As has been shown, the best course to answer how Canadian Pentecostal clergy are affected in their spiritual practices by trauma will be revealed through the three lenses of practical theology, practice-led research, and the phenomenological method. Practical theology offers Osmer's four tasks, as outlined earlier in this chapter, which will allow us to answer his four questions: "What is going on? Why is this going on? What ought to be going on? How might we respond?"[46] In practice-led research, we investigate a problem that has arisen in the researcher's practice. Since I have been deeply affected by trauma both before and during my role as clergy, I realize that it has caused a negative effect on my spirituality that I was not prepared for. The researcher's own trauma led the researcher to want to study the effects of trauma on clergy spirituality to see if there is a possible way to establish better spiritual praxis during and after trauma. Finally, Van Manen's phenomenology allows the researcher to gather data so that we can deeply explore the meaning of trauma in the clergy interviewed; this allows

45. A copy of the approval letter may be seen here https://www.dropbox.com/s/jidu9rn2h1rb78l/MERB%20approval.pdf?dl=0.

46. Osmer, *Practical Theology*, 4.

the themes from each interview to be drawn out and the essence of "the thing" to be better understood.

Chapter 4 explores the data obtained through the interviews with the eleven candidates; this critical reflection on the data highlights both the emerging themes and identifies the data that may be missing from the study. As themes are drawn out, the researcher reflects on the emergent understanding of trauma that arises from both the themes and the established theories of trauma. The utilization of both has allowed for a better understanding of how trauma affects clergy. While established theories are utilized, chapter 4 mainly uncovers the deep intricacies of trauma experienced by the participants, not through the usage of outside source material but through the words, especially those that are evocative, of the participants themselves. Doing this allows the essence of the trauma to be made more apparent to the researcher, participants, and readers alike. Established theories on trauma are used more in chapter 5 when the study reflects theologically on the issues.

4

The Essence of Trauma in Pentecostal Clergy

DURING THE LITERATURE REVIEW, it was outlined how trauma impacted the person both physically and emotionally. This chapter will examine the traumatic experiences of Canadian Pentecostal clergy. A qualitative study was conceived and implemented using the phenomenological method outlined in chapter 3. This qualitative study aims to develop a descriptive statement of trauma by utilizing how the participants described it through the phenomenological interview process. Van Manen's ideal in phenomenology is to better understand the essence of the thing: "Ultimately the project of phenomenological reflection and explication is to effect a more direct contact with the experience as lived."[1] Data analysis will follow the methods of revealing the lifeworld as outlined in chapter 3 by examining the four existentials which compose the lifeworld—lived body, lived space, lived time, and lived other (or relationships)—doing this will allow the utilization of the detailed reading approach so that thematic analysis may take place in which the essences of the phenomenon can come to the surface.[2]

The chapter will begin with a description of my experience with trauma, which is an essential step in the process; Van Manen suggests that

---

1. Van Manen, *Researching Lived Experience*, 78.
2. Van Manen, *Phenomenology of Practice*, 320–23.

our personal experience with the phenomenon is the "ego-logical starting point for phenomenological research."[3] The second phase of this chapter will provide a brief overview of the eleven research participants. The third step is an examination of the process for data validation. The most significant portion of this chapter happens in the fourth step, which will describe the participants' experience or essence of trauma as revealed in the phenomenological interviews. This section will further be broken down into the seven fundamental aspects of trauma as revealed in the interview and analysis process. The usual spiritual practices revealed during the interviews will be discussed, with consideration given to how the trauma affected them. The last section of this chapter will explore a synthesis of the phenomenon by developing an anecdotal narrative of the seven essences of trauma derived from the interviews.

PERSONAL EXPERIENCE WITH TRAUMA

The two defining characteristics of this project are that it is rooted in practical theology and practice-led research. These two factors highlight the importance of my study in that it is derived from within my practice. As a clergy member who has been licensed or ordained with the Pentecostal Assemblies of Canada since 1991, I have personal experience with trauma and how it has affected me while in ministry. I have experienced varying levels of trauma during these years, but I will highlight one specific event which has shaped me. The following is a recounting of my most significant experience with trauma.

> On March 9th, 1999, while in between church positions, I was working in the office of a car parts manufacturer. My family consisted of my wife, two young daughters, and an infant son who was almost four months old. I had arisen around 6 am to prepare for work and checked on the children to ensure they were covered and still sleeping. I entered the room my daughters shared and readjusted their covers as they had kicked them off in the middle of the night. I then went into my infant son's room to check on him, and as I adjusted his blankets, he did not move, which was unusual. I quickly realized that he was not breathing, and I pulled him from his cradle, called for my wife, and started cardio-pulmonary resuscitation (CPR). My wife tried to call 911 but was frantic, so I quickly dialed that number as I continued CPR. While we were

---

3. Van Manen, *Researching Lived Experience*, 54.

only a few blocks from the hospital, the ambulance seemed to take an eternity to arrive, even though it had arrived relatively quickly. When the ambulance arrived, the paramedics took over the CPR, and the next thing I knew, I was in the back of the ambulance with my son on our way to the hospital, as my wife stayed with our daughters. I was taken into the treatment room area at the hospital while they took my son behind a closed door to try and help him.

I remember hearing the distinct ticking sound of the analog clock reverberating above the room's silence. I prayed, "God, please make Dawson better." While the sound of the clock ticked on, showing that time was progressing, for me, it was as if I was stuck at this moment. Eventually, a doctor would emerge from the room where they were working on my son, and at that moment, all my hope was gone as I saw tears in her eyes, and I heard her utter the words "I am so sorry." She had said other things, but none of them I remember as my grief overwhelmed my ability even to comprehend her. Now I was faced with telling my wife that our son had died.

Thoughts of "Why God? Why God? Why God? How could you let this happen?" ran through my mind. I questioned His goodness and love for me; I felt alone and believed He had abandoned me. As these thoughts raced through my mind, I immediately felt guilty for entertaining them. When I told my wife, her grief and the grief of our young daughters were added to my own.

The ensuing days would be a whirlwind of activity; we would have to arrange a funeral, and we would be interviewed by the police detectives, who would try and determine whether there was something nefarious that we had done to cause this death.[4] The funeral was just a wave of people around me trying to care for and comfort me in my grief, but I was lost in the crowd in my mind. I remember very little of the actual funeral, but I noticed that people got on with their lives in the days and weeks following the funeral, and I wondered how they could do that when I was so obviously hurting. I wondered if they cared that I was hurting; did it even matter to them?[5]

---

4. This was standard operating procedure for an unexplained death at home for the Woodstock, On police department.

5. This account was recreated through memory and some journal notes taken shortly after the experience.

Reflecting on that experience, I realize there is much to investigate. First, while applying CPR on my son, I felt that time was not moving; my reality in regard to the passage of time had changed, and I could no longer differentiate what was accurate. This same feeling was repeated while waiting in the treatment area while the medical staff worked on my son. The clock ticked but only represented a sound; in my experience, time had stopped moving. I experienced trauma through a lens that reality was now less concrete and was more subjective depending on my feelings. Second, the overwhelming grief I was experiencing caused me to shut out and shut off external stimuli, but it still allowed me to see emotions. For example, when the doctor informed me of the prognosis, I heard and remembered very few of her words. I do not remember her name, although I know she told me. However, I vividly remember the tears in her eyes and the nervousness she was experiencing as she told me about Dawson's fate. Third, my trauma was experienced through grief, which would be expected in the death of a child. However, it was further exacerbated by also experiencing grief through my wife and daughters' eyes, which is vicarious trauma. Fourth, the questioning by the police, while I understood it was standard procedure, made me feel that I was being attacked and blamed for what happened to my son. The interview process led to feeling alone in that room and alone in my experience. This feeling of being alone further manifests itself when I wonder how people can continue with their lives while I am still hurting. Finally, questioning God was an essential aspect of how I experienced trauma. Although I was theologically trained as a Pentecostal pastor, I had no training on how to react to this or understand why God would allow it to happen. Feelings of guilt became encompassing as I continued to question God and His providence.

RESEARCH PARTICIPANTS

When conducting qualitative research, the question often arises of how many research participants are enough to gain data saturation.[6] Since phenomenology is utilized in this research and is a qualitative methodology,

---

6. Data saturation in qualitative research is the point at which no new data is being retrieved during your research, and everything garnered from this point on is a repetition of data retrieved from previous interview. For example, if you interview 10 people and then notice at person 6 onward, that the information you are receiving from the interviews is a repetition of the previous interviews, then you have achieved data saturation.

it should also answer this question. So then, it should be noted that the framework I am using borrows from that of Max Van Manen, who does not believe that data saturation exists in phenomenology. Van Manen says data saturation "does not make sense when doing phenomenology. It may be helpful in other types of qualitative inquiries, but phenomenological understanding is not a matter of filling up some kind of qualitative container until it is full."[7] Van Manen's point is that when you ask the phenomenological question, you have opened up a question with no bottom; there is no point in which the question returns all the meanings of the phenomenon. This study then aimed to find a suitable number of research participants with different experiences to interview, which would produce varied data. In addition, the concept of a magic number has been dropped in most fields of qualitative research, including phenomenology, especially that of Van Manen.[8] This project then searched not for a certain number of participants but rather for various candidates whose experiences were rich in the phenomenon so that a wide range of essences could emerge.

As noted in the previous chapter, the study asked for participants among the clergy of two Pentecostal denominations in Canada—PAOC & PAONL—who self-identified as having gone through an experience that brought on a traumatic response.[9] Geographical diversity was established though having representation for every region of the country except the Territories and Quebec.

The gender makeup of the study consisted of eight males and three females who agreed to participate and met the requirements of this study. This gender breakdown was representative of the percentages of male vs. female clergy in the denominations under consideration.[10] The participants ranged from thirty-one to sixty-six years of age—all of the subjects

7. Van Manen et al., "Conversation," 5.

8. Webb, *Qualitative Dissertation?*, 101–3. Webb does not strictly speak on phenomenology, as his book is about qualitative research in general. He does use the concept of data saturation, which Van Manen suggests is not applicable to phenomenology. Webb however does suggest a "rule of thumb" for his preferred number of candidates in qualitative research being eight to twelve.

9. This study was reviewed by the McMaster University Research Ethics Board (MREB) and received ethics clearance. A copy of the clearance, as well as all scripts used in recruitment, can be seen in the appendices of this project.

10. *PAOC Fellowship Stats*, 3. Females represented approximately 27 percent of subjects in this study which is aligned with the percentage of female credential holders in the PAOC. No stats were available for the PAONL. Two more females came forward to participate in the study but were disqualified because of restrictions in place by the MREB.

identified as Caucasian.[11] The clergy represented churches, which varied in size and average weekly attendance, ranging from twenty-five to four hundred plus people. The clergy also represented an excellent rural and urban/suburban mix. Most of the participants were in active ministry, except one who has recently retired due to medical issues. The diversity represented by these participants allowed for a multidimensional picture of the phenomenon to emerge.

Regarding the interviews, each used phenomenological methodology and was open-ended. The interviews ranged from 31 minutes to 101 minutes in length.[12] After obtaining biographical data, the phenomenological interview began with a broadly scoped query: "Please share with me a specific experience in which you have experienced trauma, and please be as detailed as possible." This question allowed each participant to reflect on the event that caused the trauma and their responses. So that a more detailed exploration of the phenomenon, the usage of exploratory questions brought the subject back to the essence of the experience. Possible exploratory questions were submitted to the MREB; some of these questions or variations were utilized to understand better how the participants experienced the phenomenon.[13]

DATA VALIDATION

Max Van Manen, whose phenomenological lens is utilized in this project, believes that data verification in phenomenology is not undertaken as it is in other qualitative and quantitative methodologies. Instead of using data verification methods like most qualitative projects use, Van Manen suggests that the phenomenologist test the project's validity; this is achieved by examining the project as a whole and asking if it is based on a valid phenomenological question about the human experience. Next, there should be validation that the analysis is done on descriptive accounts, not those primarily containing opinions. Following that, the researcher

---

11. One of the participants who was disqualified by the MREB was a person of color. Unfortunately, no other persons of color came forward for the study.

12. The mean interview length was 48 minutes; the median interview length was 40 minutes. All values were rounded to the closest minute during tabulation.

13. These questions are available in the appendices titled "Interview Questions." They were not used verbatim but would be modified depending on the direction the interview was naturally taking.

must ascertain that the study relies on primary and scholarly sources of phenomenological literature and avoids importing methods of validation that are not in phenomenology.[14] All preceding steps were undertaken in this research to validate the project. In addition, a summary statement of each interview and a general summary of the significant trauma essences were sent to the participants to verify that the researcher understood their story. This final step occurred so there would be no confusion over what the researcher thought was said and that which was actually said. The participants emailed back their comments or had a short meeting via Zoom with the researcher to discuss the summaries. While not everyone chose to respond, those who did respond agreed with the personal and general summaries. Based on implementing these strategies, I am therefore convinced of the austerity and efficacy of the data produced by the qualitative study.

THE ESSENCE OF THE PHENOMENON OF TRAUMA

The description of the phenomenon of trauma will be presented by highlighting the seven most significant essences gleaned from the interviews and their subsequent analysis. As shown in chapter 3, significance was established by determining the prevalence of the essences as they appeared across the interviews. If an essence appeared in more interviews, it was assigned more priority. Next, greater importance was given if there was a high frequency of appearances of an essence across all the interviews. In this case, the seven essences represent 86 percent of the total number of essences across all documents, whereas the other seventeen ones that are not highlighted represent the other 14 percent. As already stated, no phenomenological study can discover every meaning of a phenomenon, so for this study, when it is said that "The essence of trauma is," that is only in regards to what was revealed during the interviews of the subjects, and is not meant to be all-encompassing in nature, although it very well may apply to many.

The Essences of Clergy Trauma

The phenomenon of trauma experienced by clergy consists of seven components that make up its essence.

1. Trauma in the clergy manifests as *anxiety*.

14. Van Manen, *Phenomenology of Practice*, 350–51.

2. Trauma in the clergy brings a sense of *loneliness.*
3. Trauma in the clergy causes a *questioning or anger with God* to occur.
4. Clergy feels that leadership is unsupportive *(unsupportive leadership.)*
5. There is a sense of *self-doubt* in clergy facing trauma.
6. Clergy experience *brain fog* during trauma.
7. Clergy experience *disempowerment* during their trauma.

The following section will provide a complete description of these seven essences of trauma, using the language of the research participants. As has been stated, but bears repeating, the recipients' accounts are anonymized and have been assigned a random name.

Trauma in the Clergy Manifests as Anxiety

During the interviews and the subsequent analysis to uncover the essences of trauma, anxiety played a large part in the experience. Participants describe this in various ways, which we will uncover in this section.

Physical Manifestations—"I was shocked, I could barely breathe" (Will)

As displayed through anxiety, physical manifestation often accompanies the experiences of trauma. Many of the participants who relayed that they felt a general sense of anxiety had physical symptoms attached to that feeling. Andrew experienced a general sense of nervousness which caused him to manifest physically, "I was extremely anxious, and I was physically pacing the floor because I am unsure how to handle this issue." Shawn's anxiety further revealed itself physically and mentally; he describes his time as something that led to "a pretty bad bout of anxiety and depression that ultimately led to me going on sick leave. I ignored the symptoms; there were pseudo heart attacks that the doctor told me were angina attacks, and I was passing out." These extreme physical symptoms were not unique to Shawn; Paula also exhibited similar symptoms. Paula recalls having anxiety attacks, something she shares she had not felt since college; anxiety for her is evidenced by "palpitations and chest tightness." On the other hand, Mark shared that although he is usually very patient with people, he is now "short-tempered and less patient with people; anger is just below the surface."

Uncertain Future—"What is on the other side?" (Shawn)

Anxiety often leads to the feeling of an uncertain future. As we see in Shawn's quote above, heightened anxiety is prevalent when there is no clear path forward. The uncertain future can also become a sense of impending doom. Will said he felt "impending doom; I felt like there was an attack coming." Part of the trauma that Les experienced revolved around choices one of his parents had made; this led to his anxiety about an uncertain future; he wondered if his parent's choices "would affect his future in ministry." These feelings of an uncertain future manifested themselves in the anxiety as an essence of the trauma. If caused by job loss, physical danger, or damage to the reputation of the sufferer caused the traumatic experience. Anxiety with the feeling of an uncertain future was often noted.

Internalized Emotions—"I felt panicky" (Jackie)

In many people experiencing trauma, anxiety is an internalized feeling. Some accompany these through outward manifestations, but this is not always the case. There were often phrases that stood alone during the interviews, which did not indicate any other physical responses to the anxiety. Andrew relays his feeling as "extremely anxious, on edge, stressful, and a sense of shock." While Paula vocalizes her anxiety as "fear, tension, and nervousness." Internalized symptoms appear in every participant who shared they felt anxiety because of their trauma. Mark declares that his internalized anxiety was through a feeling of shock. He states that "everything was like just, that shock."

Heightened Awareness—"I am not letting my guard down" (Connie)

Those interviewed displayed another significant way anxiety presents itself in the trauma suffers: they have a sense of heightened awareness. In this, they are on constant guard for situations that may cause a traumatic event's repetition. Using Jackie's interview as an example, she displays that her anxiety from trauma caused heightened awareness when she decided to sever a relationship that had been the cause of trauma. She states, "I severed the relationship through a letter because I just could not handle dealing with him." There is also tension between being guarded and still wanting to remain open. Andrew shares this tension when he declares, "I was guarded, but I wanted to be more open. I wanted to let people in because maybe I wanted to let them see what happened, and I wanted some sympathy or empathy and reassurance that I wasn't crazy, but I was guarded because I could not handle another major hurt." For Paula, guardedness extends to those she cares for as well. She describes her desire to protect her family and those who were cared for under her ministry and then declares, "the protective instinct of just okay, what is going to create the most safety, and that is the guardedness that comes from that."

Trauma in The Clergy Brings a Sense of Loneliness

The experience of loneliness was essential to how the participants felt their trauma. Jason shared, "In some ways, the hardest thing was not having the people around that I can talk to, share with what went down." This underlying sense of loneliness revealed itself in varying ways in the separate individuals. The following section will uncover the three ways this essence manifested itself in the individuals, using the participants' words. Generally, the people who expressed the feeling of loneliness also expressed the idea that they lost the feeling of community in the process, or there is no established sense of community available to clergy due to extenuating circumstances. Exploring these ideas will be done in three parts; the first will be about loneliness because of a lack of a confidant. The second will explore how participants felt lonely because people abandoned them. The third will examine the tendency of the person experiencing trauma to pull inward.

LACK OF A CONFIDANT—"THERE WAS NO ONE SAFE" (PAULA)

The job of the clergy member is to minister, not to be the recipient of the ministry themselves. That idea was commonly shared during the interview stage of the research. Connie, for example, gives this ideal when she says, "It can also be because you are isolated, you know, it is just something you cannot share. It is not my job to go through something and have people minister to me." Paula expresses this feeling by saying that "there was really nobody safe to talk to or be present with." Clergy often face their burdens alone because of a separation in roles between clergy and laity. Clergy are to be the caregivers, not the care receivers. Paula says, "So there was not much community, either in terms of presence and spending time with people or discussing the actual situation. So, there was no opportunity to use any of those things without compromising integrity." Professionalism in the ministry, or integrity, as Paula refers to it, prevents clergy from seeking help from those with whom they have fostered relationships within their parishes.

In addition to the clergy/laity divide in care, which leads to loneliness, there is also an aspect where clergy do not feel safe talking to other clergy. One participant described it as a sense of competition between clergy members, which led to this feeling. Kirk declares that "but our clergy, our fellow pastors are typically our competitors, we do not treat each other with good relationships, with transparent relationships." For some, the competition between clergy can bring about a feeling of not having a safe space to share amongst colleagues. While she had a good relationship with some fellow clergy, Paula expressed that she could not be fully open with them, "because of the denominational relationship, you do not want to disclose too much." To her, it was an issue that sharing her problems with this other clergy would put this clergy member in an awkward position within the denomination.

Rejection—"I am totally shunned" (Andrew)

Rejection is a crucial symptom in the clergy who experience trauma, leading to a deepening sense of loneliness. In addition to the role as clergy, Shawn worked in non-church employment. He experienced rejection in the non-church position; he recalls people calling him a racist and bigot, making for a toxic work environment. "There were days I walked into work, and I would have to go through all of the head office and then close my door because I could not stand seeing anybody." Shawn's experience is from outside the church, whereas Will's feeling of rejection comes from inside the church. Will felt that his experience that led to trauma caused a severing of pre-existing relationships within the church he was pastoring, and through it, he "lost a lot of friends." Jason felt his traumatic situation caused people not to want to associate with him; "So I felt they did not want me around because of this, of what we were going through because of the struggle we were going through." The concept of being pushed aside or shunned causes this deep sense of being alone in the person. Andrew, as seen above, reckoned it with being shunned. He further explains this by saying, "we felt totally cut off. Like there was no one from the church that reached out to us. They did not reach out to us to say, Hey, what happened? Or even, how are you doing?" While this feeling runs counter to the separation between clergy and laity, it reveals that the clergy still want to know that people care about them.

Self Isolation—"I did not want to hang around with people" (Mark)

The loneliness experienced by trauma suffers can sometimes be self-inflicted. There were often incidents where the participants described a logical conundrum of wanting to know people cared but not wanting to be around people. In quotes earlier in this section, Andrew expresses his dismay because people have not reached out to him to see how he is doing, but in the same thought, Andrew expresses being okay with being away from people. Before he wondered why people were not contacting him, he said, "We were okay to pull, I guess you might say, inward toward ourselves, and we wanted to break ties for a while." Jason shared that his feeling of people rejecting him because of his trauma "caused me to isolate myself, which did not help." Connie shares that her shame caused her to isolate herself, "And I never told anybody. So, I Isolated alone, living with shame and then trying to heal my family and all of that." Kirk viewed his withdrawal from people as a benefit to him, "I withdrew actually from connecting with people in the church, which meant that I had a little bit more time." He used this time to pray, worship, and connect with God more. Kirk was the only one to link his isolation with a chance to have deeper connections with God.

On the other hand, Mark did not want to be around people because he could not emotionally deal with any problems they might bring him; "I just could not be around people and deal with other people's needs. People will come to you with a need and I felt like saying, buddy, that is not a need; just smarten up." Whatever the reason is, the subjects had a strong tendency to pull inward, even if they also expressed a desire to have people show concern.

Trauma in the Clergy Causes a Questioning or Anger with God to Occur

People who have a deep interest in things of faith, especially clergy, will often examine things through the lens of that faith. Clergy who have experienced trauma do this by expressing anger or questioning God. They wonder where God is in the midst of their trouble; they express anger that God seems not to care. This section will explore three key areas that the research participants expressed during the interviews: first, the concept of questioning God amid their trauma. Second, the participants were angry with God. Third, the participants expressed that they withdrew from God because of their trauma.

Angry with God—"I was crying and yelling at God" (Les)

Christians do not often feel comfortable being angry with or even questioning God. Some of the participants in the study shared this sentiment. They would express some element of being angry with God while making excuses for God in the next breath. Les, for example, shared that he was angry and yelling at God; when prompted with the question of whether he thought this was a valid spiritual practice, his reply was, "I am going to say yes with hesitation, 'cause I think that we need to respect God. There needs to be reverence, but God also created us with these emotions." We see that while Les experienced trauma as anger towards God, but he also had to justify this response. In Mark we find another example of anger towards God, "So the anger, there were times that you are really angry, I get in the car, and I would yell and scream at myself, or God or whatever." Mark also made excuses for God and downplayed his anger towards Him by saying, "The weird thing was, I do not know if I was angry at God because I have a pretty strong view that we are responsible for our own actions." As Mark continued his explanation, he brought his anger toward God into more of an idea of questioning God; This shows that anger towards God and questioning Him can be indistinguishable. For some participants, there are no excuses made for God; Connie's simple statement says, "I am angry at God." Whereas Andrew's feelings towards God were "I am hurt, and I am angry, but at the same time, I felt it was okay for me. Not that I would, like, I was never at the point where I would ever shake my fist at God and curse God and die. Lord, I am upset. I am upset with you. I don't know why this is happening?" While some qualify their anger and others do not, the underlying fact remains that anger towards God is how people of faith often express their trauma.

The Essence of Trauma in Pentecostal Clergy

Why God?—"It made me question how much God loved me" (Connie)

Questioning of God and anger with God is often expressed by clergy experiencing trauma. While they are often coupled and are an individual essence for this study, exploring some significant differences is in order. Questioning of God by the participants can vary from questioning where He is during troublesome times to wondering about God's love for the person in trauma. Andrew wondered, "does God hear me, are my prayers just hitting the ceiling? You know what is going on here?" For him, he was not questioning God but wondering whether God even heard him. On the other hand, Connie showed that she was questioning God directly; "I did spend time asking, saying I do not get it. God. Why? I like questioning why I do not get it. I do not get how this can happen." Connie, however, still had feelings similar to Andrew's, questioning God's presence or care for her. She declared that the trauma made her question "how much God loved me. I just do not get it, God; why would you do this to me? Like, what did I do that was so wrong?" To Will, it was not about questioning God's existence but rather why this was happening. In his exasperation from the trauma, he declared, "I've had my fill. I'm done. So, I never questioned God. Or asked if He is real? Or is he not faithful? But the questions like, why am I going through this? I don't sense the pure joy of trials of many kinds right now." The questioning of God then is experienced as either directly questioning God in asking Him why they are going through the problem or questioning whether God is aware of their predicament.

Withdrawal from God—"I was withdrawing from God" (Danny)

If someone is angry at God or feels that God does not care, it can lead to the person withdrawing from the relationship with God. Connie shared that her trauma affected her; she felt it was "a battle I'm still fighting, and I fight to keep my faith and fight to not let the thoughts in my head affect my relationship." Trauma in Danny affected how he viewed Christ, the Church, and Christians in general; "It wore us down to the point where after a while it just impacted; it impacted our view of the Church, Christianity, Jesus, Christians." Jason said he was isolating himself from God even though he knew he needed to be in His presence more; "I was isolating myself from

God. What I needed was to be more in his presence." While the trend was that most people suggested they withdrew from God, there was some evidence of people who found solace in getting closer to God in their trauma, even if they expressed anger or questions toward Him.[15] The view held by Kirk and Shawn was that while they questioned or were angry with God, they drew solace from coming to Him in their spiritual practices. Shawn, for example, said he "started digging into scriptures, you know, stories of people going through adversity."

Unsupportive Leadership is an Essence of Trauma

The fourth essence of trauma uncovered in the interview and analysis stages was that the participants felt that leadership was unsupportive. When considering essence two, where the participants felt a sense of loneliness, sometimes related to a lack of confidants, this essence compounds that feeling of loneliness. Examination of unsupportive leadership will happen in this section in two primary ways. First, the respondents highlighted that they felt denominational leadership did not support them; these incidents are immediately accented and brought into view. Second, a category of leaders who were not denominational leaders is revealed as unsupportive; quotes from the interviews will be presented to further reveal the incidents. As an additional point, some participants mentioned that this lack of support by leadership, especially denominational, affected their view of those leaders or positions; these will be noted in the two categories discussed in this section.

Unsupportive Denominational Leadership—"The district was not helpful" (Paula)

The predominant way this essence revealed itself was through the feeling that denominational leadership, sometimes called the district, was not supportive. In Andrew's account, he generally felt unsupported by denominational leadership. He admits they heard him, but in the end, "There was no action taken. There was really no one to go to." Paula also recounts that she

---

15. Creswell and Poth, *Qualitative Inquiry*, 341. Creswell and Poth share that pointing out the negative case analysis, where the data does not always conform to the standard seen in others, is a way of providing a "realistic assessment of the phenomenon under study. In real life, not all evidence is either positive or negative; it is some of both."

felt that district leadership was not supportive after they became aware of the situation; she did not receive "much response or support from district leadership."

Others felt that denominational leadership took an adversarial role in their situations. During the event that caused his trauma, Kirk recalls that the denominational leadership came in, and they seemed to be against him, "I can't try to sort out this church and sort out the district. Like you're not coming on my side. You're not even an equal person here. You're bypassing the board." That experience changed his view of the denomination's leadership, "I was looking for support from the district superintendent. And that experience showed me that I can't look to the district superintendent for support."

Will also shares that the perceived lack of support by denominational leadership caused him not to trust them; "we don't trust our denomination like we did before, we feel that more strongly because of their lack of assistance or wisdom in the situation that we just went through." With Les, he felt his district superintendent laughed at his problems, making him feel "very overwhelmed and unsupported." Denominational leadership's lack of perceived support caused the trauma sufferer to have a diminished view of those leaders. The denomination, according to Les, was "sacrificing a pastor." Les also feels that it is the district's role to support the pastor and their lack of acting in this capacity means that "there is no safe relationship for the pastors when they get into a crisis." Mark's recollection of how the denomination was unsupportive, said he "felt like damaged goods." He also questioned why the denomination was not there during his crisis.

Local Leader Unsupportive—"Threatened to be fired" (Les)

There were also incidents where the person who experienced trauma felt that other leaders, outside of denominational leadership, also lacked in giving them support. In many of these cases, the clergy were not the church's Lead Pastor but served as support pastors. Les was in such a position that he was "threatened to be fired six times." Andrew was also working in a support pastor role when the Lead Pastor decided to call him into a meeting; he recalls that it felt like being "pulled into the principal's office and was, you know, basically reprimanded." In both cases mentioned above, the participants had a diminished view of the leaders involved.

Self-doubt Is an Essence of Trauma

"Maybe there is something wrong with me." (Danny) Phrases similar to that appeared in the interviews and during analysis. They reveal trauma as an insidious predator that hunts not only the outside of the sufferer but also pushes deep into the person's *psyche*. This section will carefully examine self-doubt, uncovering the four ways the participants experienced it. First, the participants experienced a sense of self-loathing. Second, they had a warped sense of personal responsibility in which they assumed blame for things outside their control. Third, they struggled with embarrassment because of their trauma and the situation which caused it. Finally, they had times when they ignored their judgement and did the opposite of what they thought was best.

Self-loathing—"I hated myself for years" (Connie)

The inner scars that affect people are the hardest for outsiders to see or understand, yet these wounds are prevalent in this essence of trauma. Connie expresses these scars by hating herself, as seen above. Jackie also expressed similar feelings as she stated that she "deserved bad things." For Danny, it affected how he viewed himself; he had self-doubts and wondered, "maybe there is something wrong with me." This essence of trauma causes the individual to doubt their self-worth. The self-loathing caused Jason to wonder whether he was even fit to be a member of the clergy; "there was the idea that, or the thought that, you know, I shouldn't even be pastoring anymore, that if we're struggling in this area, you know, am I even fit to be a pastor." Trauma devalues the individual in their own eyes, believing that is how others see them. Connie shared several experiences where members of her congregation wondered if why the trauma happened was her fault. She recalls people saying, "Connie, can I just ask you, was it something you did? And I went, I wouldn't be in this position as a pastor if it was something I did. But yeah, I had the people who went fishing, the fishing expedition." Danny also shared that people would see him as he saw himself; he believed that "no other church would want me." Will wondered, "Man am I going crazy." As shown, the feelings of self-loathing can come in varied ways, but the phenomenon is real regardless of how experienced.

The Essence of Trauma in Pentecostal Clergy

Warped Sense of Personal Responsibility—"Everything was my fault" (Jackie)

The interview participants who shared a sense of self-doubt often did this through the expression that they were responsible for things outside their control. For example, Jackie said she had a "warped sense of personal responsibility. Everything was my fault, even stuff that wasn't my fault." Trauma caused many subjects to view themselves negatively, so they often blamed the trauma on themselves. Danny expressed, "I was trying to figure out why and you know, well maybe there is something that I've done." Connie said she felt that she "had failed my daughter and failed myself." Even though the circumstances surrounding the incident that caused her trauma was outside of her control. Les said he experienced "a lot of guilt because I didn't speak up then when that was the time that I should have." While he feels this sense of responsibility, as shared in the interview, his story reveals that he did speak up on several occasions about problems he was experiencing.

Embarrassed—"I isolated alone living with shame" (Connie)

In the section on self-loathing, the subjects often shared that they felt others viewed them the way they perceived themselves. That was a factor which contributed to the idea that self-doubt expresses itself in embarrassment and shame. Danny, whose trauma origins are in a church conflict, said, "You're embarrassed, you're embarrassed for the church, you're embarrassed for yourself." He expresses embarrassment when he says he is "wondering what people are thinking. You are out in the community just doing your stuff, and you're kind of wondering if people know what is going on." For those in trauma, their self-image becomes tainted, which leads to a sense of embarrassment and shame. They believe this causes them to be unworthy of respect, which we see in Jason's query, "Am I even fit to be a pastor?"

Go Against Personal Judgment—"I went against my own judgment"

Going against what you know to be right was also expressed by the participants in the study. Will, whose trauma was because of a congregation member who abused him, shared, "And I just, I want to do what I can to maintain a brother in Christ, walk with forgiveness and walk with grace and be, and do what I preach of grace and forgiveness. And you know, every time again, looking back on, even telling you now, I feel so stupid because it's classic pattern of abuse." Will ignored his judgement of the situation, ignoring the abuse, and instead sought to restore the man. While this can be a conundrum for the Christian, they are to forgive; there also needs to be an understanding that personal safety is paramount. Connie, whose trauma was caused due to the lack of safety of a loved one, said she went "against her better judgement." Trauma revealed itself, causing the sufferer to ignore typical warning signs when they present themselves.

Clergy Experience Brain Fog During Trauma

The participants of the interviews also expressed that an essence of their trauma was the experience of brain fog. There were four primary ways this was revealed, and each one will be explored in more detail using the subjects' language. First, they shared that they were experiencing a general state of confusion. Second, they sometimes had a difficult time distinguishing what was real. Third, the trauma caused them to be unable to maintain focus. Fourth, this made them unsure of what was happening around them.

Confusion—"So many confusing thoughts" (Danny)

Confusion can manifest itself in a variety of ways and also connect itself to other feelings. Andrew links his confusion to the essence of isolation when he declares, "it was also very confusing because we didn't understand, or at least I didn't understand why no one from the church board or from the church even want to know what actually happened that would cause such a drastic decision to be made." Andrew's confusion also caused a lack of clarity; he said, "I was just very confused, and it did affect my thinking, and I lacked clarity." Danny expresses this same lack of clarity when he states, "But I think there were so many confusing thoughts about all that was going on, there wasn't my normal clarity of, and clearness of mind." The participants shared that the lack of clarity affected their everyday activities, with Paula saying, "Ok God, this is on you!" However, immediately after saying this, she admitted that her "thoughts were very scattered."

The Essence of Trauma in Pentecostal Clergy

What Is Real?—"Is this all just made up?" (Mark)

Not only did the participants share that they had a general sense of confusion during the trauma experience, but there were also times when they could not distinguish reality from fantasy. Jackie said she "found it really hard to decipher what was true or reasonable, and that's not me; I'm very logic focused." The brain fog brought on by trauma for her then changed her usual demeanour. Mark shared several times that he thought he was in a dream during his trauma. In one instance, he says, "everything that was real became fake, and reality seemed like a dream. So, it felt like I was in a dream." He said it even made him wonder, "Am I going to wake up? Is this all just made up?"

Lack of Focus—"I didn't know what was going on" (Kirk)

In the essence of brain fog, many of the subsections that are highlighted overlap with each other. While the lack of focus and the concept of confusion could have been joined, the interviews relayed a more profound reaction than just general confusion. One example of this is in Will's interview, where he shares that not only did he lack focus, but he was surprised it did not affect his regular duties as a pastor; "Hard to focus, hard to focus, like looking back on it, I don't know how I could preach on Sunday." Mark had a similar experience where he can not focus, affecting his routine: "I felt like I was babbling because I could not think straight, I couldn't get my thoughts clear, I couldn't study." The emotive words that were shared to relay a state of confusion varied; for Paula, her "thoughts were scattered," While Danny generalizes it as him having a "lack of clarity, I was in a fog." Regardless of the words utilized to express this feeling, the participants often shared confusion as an aspect of the phenomenon.

What Is Going On?—"I don't understand" (Kirk)

It should again be stated that the four subcategories in this essence are highly related. The differences often lie in the degree of the experience. In this subcategory, the subjects felt they did not understand what was going on. Of course, this can be linked to the general confusion. However, when this idea presented itself during analysis, a more profound expression manifested other than general confusion. Kirk details that his general feeling of not understanding compounded into something more profound, "The only memory I have is that I don't understand. I don't understand. I don't understand. And it actually got to a point where I didn't know what was going on." In that account, we see the progression from a generalized confusion into a more profound state of not understanding. Jackie says that those moments for her became "so disorienting, and you're just like, I don't even know what is happening anymore."

Clergy Experience Disempowerment During Trauma

Disempowerment is experienced in a variety of ways. Four profound ways to experience disempowerment are noted during the interviews and subsequent analysis. First, the trauma sufferer can feel belittled. Second, there was a sense that they felt they had lost control. Third, they believed they were victims of intimidation. Fourth, they felt their reputation was challenged or at stake. The following sections will cover each of these using the words of the participants to highlight their significance.

BELITTLED—"I WAS BELITTLED FOR EXPRESSING EMOTION" (JACKIE)

The fifth essence of trauma revealed a sense of self-loathing, and embarrassment was often felt. Those feelings were exacerbated when they thought other people might view them in the same negative light in which they viewed themselves. This subsection touches upon a similar premise; however, the stimuli for this come from an external source, not an internal one. Jackie shares that her abuser made her feel belittled, even to the point that the person would belittle her for "expressing emotion." Andrew shares his job loss caused a sense of being "emasculated because I could no longer provide for my family." When Les was being reprimanded by his denominational representative, he said he felt "small and belittled." In each of those scenarios, the attack on their personhood occurred because of the actions of another person or thing.

The Essence of Trauma in Pentecostal Clergy

Losing Control—"I'm stuck, and I can't move forward, I feel helpless" (Kirk)

When the research participants experienced disempowerment, sometimes it was expressed as a loss of control or a feeling of helplessness. Jackie's trauma was caused by dealing with an abusive person; she shared that she became overwhelmed and "was crying and losing control." She had previously stated that this behaviour was unlike her typical personality traits. With Kirk, he becomes stuck in that moment, unable to move forward, and he "feels helpless." Paula revealed her feeling of helplessness when she declared, "I don't know how long I can do this."

Intimidated—"There was constant criticism of everything" (Paula)

The clergy member in the throes of trauma also expressed feelings of intimidation. Danny, for example, stated that the person who was the cause of trauma would try and intimidate him by "sitting out front of my house." In one recounting that Andrew gives, he speaks words that reveal his feelings about how the Lead Pastor viewed him; "So the next week it was like I got pulled into the proverbial principal's office and was reprimanded." Danny's trauma made him feel like he was being treated as a child. In Paula's case, the intimidation came through waves of what she refers to as constant criticism; "Very constant criticism of everything, from personal ambitions, or that I wanted to buy a house, or even the way I spoke to my husband." These interactions gave her a sense of unease and towards the people who leveled these accusations.

Reputation Challenged—"You are trying to discredit me" (Paula)

The respondents in this section highlight that they experienced disempowerment from people who were challenging their reputations. Danny, who was experiencing trauma because of a church conflict where people were attacking him, said that he felt his "reputation was being challenged." Paula, on the other hand, sensed that people were mocking her. According to Paula, the mocking was an attempt to "discredit me. Or try to damage my credibility." Even Andrew's story of being "pulled into the proverbial principal's office" can be viewed as a form of challenging one's reputation.

Phenomenological Description Summary

The descriptions of the seven essences of trauma using the words of the research participants have been highlighted above. Figure 5 summarizes these descriptions using the key phrase(s) of the essence in the left column and the features or emotive words that describe the phenomenon in the right column.

Spiritual Practices and Theological Insights from Interviews

Each participant was asked to provide biographical data during the interview process, which was previously mentioned, but in addition to this, the subjects were asked to explain their regular spiritual practices before the trauma occurred. After they discussed their trauma, each subject was then asked to reflect on their spiritual practices as they appeared during trauma to highlight if there were any significant changes. This section is not phenomenological; instead, it is for obtaining raw data on their spiritual practices. In addition, the subjects occasionally brought their theological insights into the conversation. These were not prompted but flowed naturally from the course of the interview. The following areas will explore the spiritual practices of the subjects, followed by an exploration of the theological insights provided.

Figure 5: Phenomenological Description Summary Chart

Essence	Features of the Essence
1. Anxiety	A) Physical Manifestations – bodily symptoms including sweating, paleness, heart racing, fainting.
	B) Uncertain Future – financial insecurity, no clear path ahead, job insecurity, impending doom, physical danger.
	C) Internalized Emotions – on edge, panicky, fear, tension, nervousness, shock
	D) Heightened Awareness – guarded, aware, hypervigilant, protective
2. Loneliness	A) No Confidant – confidentiality concerns, competition with other clergy, protect clergy/laity relationship
	B) Rejection – toxicity, loss of friends, abandoned, shunned, cut off
	C) Self Isolation – pull inward, shame induced isolation, short-tempered with others
3. Questioning/Anger with God	A) Anger Towards God – yelling, angry, swearing, hurt, upset
	B) Questioning of God – why God? do you hear me? I don't get it God. how can this happen? do you love me?
	C) Withdrawal from God – fighting to keep my faith, impacted my view of God,
4. Unsupportive Leadership	A) Unsupportive Denomination – not supportive, no action taken, no response, adversary, we don't trust them, they sacrifice pastors, damaged goods, diminished view of denomination
	B) Unsupportive Local Leadership – threatened, fired, reprimanded, diminished view of leader

Spiritual Practices of the Participants Before Trauma

The subjects were asked to highlight their usual spiritual practices during the interviews. They were instructed only to mention the practices they did at least several times weekly. In total, eleven different practices were mentioned, with only two of those being universal: prayer and Bible reading. The other practices and how many interviews included them are in Figure 6. Three practices mentioned in the chart will be specifically reviewed: prayer, Bible, and connecting with others. These three are highlighted because they contain the most informative data, while the other practices were mentioned without much descriptive language. Also, the first two are universal and deserve examination, while connecting with others has tie-ins to prayer.

Figure 6: Spiritual Practices Chart

Spiritual Practice	# of Documents
Prayer	11
Bible	11
Reading Theological Books	4
Listening to Sermons/Podcasts	2
Connect with People	2
Worship	2
Journaling	1
Attend Church	2
Family Devotions	2
Job	1
Volunteering	1

During the examination of the times in which people said prayer was a normative spiritual practice, it was noted that prayer might also include meditative moments. They say they listen for God's voice and seek His direction during these moments. For example, Danny shares his prayer time when he is "Just being quiet and trying to hear the voice of God and asking God questions, in terms of what does this mean? What's going on, what should I do?" Danny's posture in prayer by listening is not a unique response from the subjects; Connie shared similar thoughts on listening to God's voice during prayer. She states, "I take that time where I'm quiet with God, where sometimes I say, okay, God, whatever you want to do, you want to talk to me? Or you want me to say something? You want me to worship or do you want me to shut up." Other subjects also said they were listening or contemplative during prayer as well; this reveals that among the subjects, prayer is not meant to be a one-way conversation with just the person praying talking, but that guidance is sought and expected from God.

Bible reading was the other universal practice from the recipients. Of the eleven people in the study, ten linked their reading of the Bible to their prayer time, and of those ten, one specifically mentioned that they spent meditative time in the Bible. Danny said, "But then I just do some other Bible reading in terms of just kind of meditating." While Danny is the only one who specifically mentioned using the Bible meditatively, this does not preclude the others from using it this way. Danny's was highlighted to show that Pentecostals use the Bible as one way to hear the voice of God.

The two subjects who highlighted connecting with people as a spiritual practice also incorporated prayer into those connection times. Kirk says his connections with other people is part of his Christian journey; "I tend to pray with other people frequently during the day, and that's part of the journey." Similarly, Shawn uses his connection with other people to pray with them and to be prayed for. He may connect with peers or people he is ministering to. When he connects with peers, he describes it like this: "I have different pastors that I connect with, talk through stuff with, whether it be personal or political or societal or ministry-related, just walking through life together." In Kirk and Shawn's discourse, we see that life as clergy is meant to be lived in connection with others.

Spiritual Practices After Trauma

There were some noticeable changes to people's spiritual practices who had experienced trauma. Some noted a change in frequency in their spiritual practices, others noted a change in intensity, while others noted new or modified spiritual practices. This section will highlight these using the words of the participants themselves.

Frequency Change

There are several points to be made in this subsection. First, some users share that they never stopped spiritual practices. Second, others say the amount of time they performed their spiritual practices increased. Thirdly, some say their spiritual practices decreased during and after trauma. There was no normative response to trauma in regard to the frequency of spiritual practices.

Danny was one example of a subject who said his spiritual practices never stopped. He credits that to "doing the work ahead of time." He means that his spiritual practices were already a habit before the trauma, so it was not hard to continue them. Mark concurs with this thought; he states regarding the frequency that his spiritual practices "wouldn't have changed because that's something I just continued on." Paula as well attributes her continued spiritual practices after trauma to her intentionality; "Those are things I was very intentional about building before. And so I didn't find that there was a change so much in the patterns." All three of the subjects noted their habits or an intentionality towards their spiritual practices before the trauma helped them to continue them during and after the trauma.

Some other participants noted that their spiritual practices increased in frequency. Kirk said that he both "prayed more and worshipped more." Shawn says that when the event which caused his trauma occurred, he noted the frequency increased where he "pressed into God with a lot of prayer." Les, who admitted he never really read the Bible before his trauma, says that now "I read the Bible daily."

On the negative side of this, Jason said that overall, his spiritual practices decreased in frequency, "my time in prayer for me was not as regular as it once was. It was like wandering around a desert."

The Intensity of Spiritual Practices

Many of the interview subjects noted that the intensity of their spiritual practices changed after trauma. Some who said they did them less frequently noted that they were more fervent when completing spiritual practices. Kirk relays this idea by saying, "I felt that I was more closely connected with God during those moments." Jason, whom we had noted in the previous subsection, had done his practices less after trauma, says, "When I did get into the Word, and I did pray, it was more intense. So, it was almost like you're wandering around the desert, and you finally find a pool of water, I'm going to drink that until it is empty." Shawn likens it to engaging his faith more profoundly, "I have never engaged my faith deeper." He continues that he found his spiritual practices to be "life-giving for me." Connie said that her trauma forced her to "cling to God because he was my next step, my next breath."

Modified or New Spiritual Practices

A few subjects either noted a new spiritual practice or a modified existing spiritual practice after experiencing trauma. For Les, he says it caused him to "work harder to rely on the Spirit." He also notes that now his trauma causes him to look for themes related to his trauma while doing Bible reading. Mark shares that he experimented with new spiritual practices during his trauma to see "which one will work." He was looking for a spiritual practice that would provide deliverance from his trauma. Jackie claimed she is logically focused and said her trauma has allowed her to now "empathize with other people, show emotion, accept and embrace and engage God's love."

Theological Insights from Interviews

During the interviews, some of the subjects provided unprompted theological insights. Two separate but linked theological positions were presented, and a very brief mention of these with quotes from the participants will be highlighted in this section.

No Room for Suffering

An idea which came up in several interviews was that there was no room for suffering from the Pentecostal theological perspective. Andrew provides this very detailed account which explains this concept well,

> I think there's not a lot of room for, you know, these dark nights of the soul and, you know, room for suffering because we're always looking for miraculous intervention. We're always looking for, you know, if we do what is right, we will be rewarded, we'll be blessed. So, if we obey and we do what's right, then God's blessing will be upon us. And, and I think that that's been something that it gets

quite ingrained into our psyche and our spirituality. But unfortunately, life circumstances are not always ideal and oftentimes very painful. And so it's as though that particular outlook or, or view maybe a worldview or theology, it doesn't stand up to the test of reality.

Will shares a similar outlook when he states, "I have a life of pain and what is pain? Like? It's kinda, you know, it's abstract at times. But I was raised in the Pentecostal church where you're supposed to live in victory all the time."

Suffering with Christ

Kirk brought in a new dimension of what he felt was happening during his trauma. For him, he was suffering with Christ, "I actually got a glimpse of what Jesus may have some part of what He may have experienced from the cross that he went to people he loved and wanted to serve, and they all lie about him." Kirk was the only one to bring this dimension in. While the Pentecostal ethos does not generally allow us to admit to suffering, as seen in quotes in the previous subsection, Kirk found some depth in his suffering outside a normative Pentecostal theology.

Lament Is Uncommon

Many of the participants shared that the practice of lament is not commonly utilized in Pentecostalism or even Evangelicalism in general. Jackie for example, shared that she finds solace in turning to worship in times of trouble but recognized that the lack of lament songs was "one of the deficiencies in praise and worship." She continued that "we have really failed to consider suffering and the beautiful things that can come out of suffering and the way that God meets us there; we have presented this very unrealistic way that we think God moves among us or he guarantees or promises us." Andrew has a similar thought process on experiencing trauma and having no avenue to express his loss when he shares, "There is not a lot of room for these dark nights of the soul and no room for suffering because we are always looking for miraculous intervention."

Anecdotal Narrative

A popular rhetorical device in qualitative or human science research, including phenomenology, is the anecdote. Van Manen shares, "Anecdote can be understood as a methodological device in human science to make comprehensible some notion that easily eludes us."[16] For this study, fictitious anecdotes are generated. The fictional account is suitable and does not draw away from its validity, as an anecdote differs in purpose from a historical account. Van Manen shares that the "historical account describes a thing that has happened in the past, but an anecdote is rather like a poetic narrative which describes a universal truth."[17] Van Manen suggests five significant functions of anecdotes in human science discourse.

First, "anecdotes form a concrete counterweight to abstract theoretical thought."[18] The purpose of phenomenology is not to generate theoretical abstractions disconnected from the reality of lived experience. Using anecdote allows phenomenology to uncover meanings that have been hidden.

Second, "anecdotes express a certain disdain for the alienated and alienating discourse of scholars who have difficulty showing how life and theoretical propositions are connected."[19] Anecdotes for the researcher and the reader to search out the relation between living and thinking.

Third, "anecdotes may provide an account of certain teachings or doctrines which were never written down."[20] Van Manen notes that the anecdotal accounts of Plato on Socrates are markedly different from the philosophical writings of the latter, which have been passed down.

Fourth, "anecdote may be encountered as concrete demonstrations of wisdom, sensitive insight, and proverbial truth."[21] In classical times, figures such as Plato considered their anecdotes as condensed narratives that contained generally acknowledged truths. Revealing these truths using anecdotes allowed for them to be more easily understood.

Fifth, "anecdotes of a certain event or incident may acquire the significance of exemplary character. Because anecdote is concrete and taken from life (in a fictional or real sense) it may be offered as an example or as

---

16. Van Manen, *Researching Lived Experience*, 116.
17. Van Manen, *Researching Lived Experience*, 119.
18. Van Manen, *Researching Lived Experience*, 119.
19. Van Manen, *Researching Lived Experience*, 119.
20. Van Manen, *Researching Lived Experience*, 119.
21. Van Manen, *Researching Lived Experience*, 120.

a recommendation for acting or seeing things in a certain way"[22] Using anecdote in this manner allows the recipient of the anecdote to perceive a truth that might be difficult to express in clear language.

Anecdotal Narratives of Trauma

In this last section of the chapter, seven fictitious anecdotes are presented, which are used to highlight how clergy experience the essences of trauma. These will each be prepared in a narrative method, with each narrative highlighting one essence; however, since essences can be interconnected, more than one may appear in the individual anecdotes.

ANXIETY

It was Monday morning, and Pastor Steve had just received a text message from a couple asking to meet later in the week. As soon as he read the message, his heart raced, and feelings of dread filled his mind. There was no indication of what the meeting was about, and when asked, the couple would not say. Steve had been a pastor at Living Waters Church for almost ten years. During his time there, the church had not grown and had actually dropped in attendance significantly, and this had caused Steve significant worry and even caused him to feel very depressed. While the people who remained were supportive of him publicly, he had overheard this same couple complaining about him after church one Sunday morning a few weeks earlier. This complaint had bothered Steve since he first heard it, and it had been on his mind much the past few weeks; he was not sleeping well and was noticeably less patient with his wife and children. The request for a meeting had put his mind into overdrive, wondering what was happening and internally worrying that he was about to lose more longtime members.

LONELINESS

Pastor Mia, who serves at Bethel Church in a remote Ontario village, was now single; two months ago, she had lost her husband of twenty years after a long bout of pancreatic cancer. They met at college, and it was love at first

---

22. Van Manen, *Researching Lived Experience*, 120.

sight. They were married between their second and third years of college. During their time as a couple, it was unusual to see one without the other; they truly loved each other's company. They were so invested in each other that she had not made close connections with many people over those years. She had no children, and her siblings, parents, and in-laws all lived at least six hours away by car. Her remote location meant that she was not even near another clergy member, save for an hour's drive. Her congregants loved her, offered support, and wanted to meet with her, but she felt that having them be her sounding board during a crisis would cross a professional and ethical line. On Sundays, she puts on a brave face, bottles up her loneliness and endeavours to serve her congregants.

Brain Fog

Five months into the year and five successive Church board meetings in which Pastor Doug was yelled at. Every meeting this year was filled with constant complaints, criticism, and animosity. In his early thirties, Doug was young compared to the church board, who were all sixty years old or older. Every meeting brought a new complaint or series of complaints. He did not understand what he was doing wrong. His mind always returned to those board meetings and the animosity shown at them. They were constantly in his thoughts, so much so that he often forgot what task he was supposed to be doing at the moment. His mind would wander off while doing tasks requiring concentration, and he would have difficulty distinguishing between what was genuine in his life and his desires. He did not know how to move forward or make the situation better.

Why God?

Hannah had been pastoring at Northview Church for three years. During that time, she and her husband had forged a bond with a young couple with two children of similar ages as their own children. The other couple's three-year-old was diagnosed with rare brain cancer one year ago. Initially, the doctors had a hopeful prognosis for the child, but as the months progressed, the prescribed treatments were not working, and the child was steadily declining. Now, she was sitting with her friends, holding their hands as the machines surrounding their child beeped. The doctors had told them there was no more they could do and that it was "in God's hands now."

Hannah was screaming on the inside, wondering how a supposedly loving God could allow this child and family to endure such a horrific disease. As the mother and her friend asked questions similar to Hannah verbally, she could not reply. Hannah, too, was caught in a place where she was angry and frustrated at God for allowing this.

Unsupportive Leadership

Darnell had just been fired from First Avenue Pentecostal Church. He was the long-time Associate Pastor at the church, but now, a new Lead Pastor, who was hired five months ago, felt Darnell was not the right fit anymore. During his time there, Darnell was responsible for Youth and Young Adults ministries. Both areas had grown in number, and the members of those groups were more engaged in their faith than ever before. The firing surprised Darnell; he was doing a good job, and the people liked him. He had poured into this church in the past six years, and now it was all gone. He was given no notice, just told to pack his office and be gone by day's end. The Lead Pastor in the five months had complained about every little thing he did not like, which Darnell had done. Darnell does not remember one time when the Lead Pastor praised him. Darnell reached out to denominational leadership for help, but they told him that there was nothing they could do. They did not meet with Darnell or call in the subsequent weeks to see how he was doing.

Disempowered

Charlie was new at this church; he has been Pastor at WellSpring Church for just one month; he had received an excellent vote to become pastor of the church, with only one person voting against him coming via anonymous ballot. Charlie now thinks he knows who that vote was, as one particular member did not take long to point out everything he thought Charlie was doing wrong. After the first Sunday, this member told Charlie, "You are not a very good preacher." Later that same week, this man came into Charlie's office and told him that he thought he would fail and be gone within a year. He would hear this man in the church's lobby criticizing and putting down everything about Charlie to other congregants. The other congregants would defend Charlie, but he still found this man's comments demeaning. Even though most of the church seemed to like Charlie, all he could think of was this one man's complaints. They made him feel small and insignificant, and felt this man was doing it to undermine Charlie's authority.

SELF-DOUBT

John had been in pastoral ministry for well over three decades. He had pastored at his current church for over half that time, and the church, while not large, had grown numerically and in spiritual engagement. He loved his congregants, and they loved him back. By all measures, he would be deemed successful in ministry. Nevertheless, one thing bothered John: his only child, his twenty-six-year-old daughter, had abandoned the faith she once cherished as a child and young adult. He wondered, "How can I be a pastor, and yet one of those closest to me does not love Jesus?" He considered leaving ministry altogether because he felt he was no longer worthy to serve God in this manner. "Maybe," he thought, "I was never really called by God, and my life has been a farce."

Summary

This chapter brought together the methodology and the biographical accounts of the participants. In doing this, a picture of the essences of clergy trauma was revealed and summarized; this allowed for a further realization of how the research participants experienced trauma. Following the summary of each essence, a fictitious narrative anecdote was produced for each essence to reveal better how those essences can look for clergy. In the next chapter, theological reflection is completed so that these essences can interact with Pentecostal theology and discover where non-Pentecostal theologies may be applied, specifically Luther's theology of the cross, so that Pentecostals will have a way to understand their trauma. Additionally, chapter 5 will show processes which will allow Pentecostals to use their trauma to grow spiritually through the implementation of the Lutheran *theologia crucis* so that when we are suffering, Christ is also suffering with us.

5

The Trauma and Triumph of the Cross

HAVING INVESTIGATED TRAUMA THROUGH scientific literature and phenomenological study, the focus now turns to the primary goal of practical theological research: theological reflection. The purpose of theological reflection is not to find yet another theory but to make a difference in the church's life. Pete Ward challenges us concerning this, "Whatever the specific format, theological reflection represents a methodological challenge. Put quite simply, how do we think about practice theologically in a way that sheds light on and then makes a difference to the ongoing life of the church?"[1] As mentioned in chapter 2, this research utilizes Richard Osmer's four tasks of practical theological interpretation so that Ward's challenge may be answered. When the study asks the question, "How can Canadian Pentecostal clergy deal with trauma while adhering to a theology of victory?" we bring the problem under examination. The descriptive-empirical task, Osmer's first task, has been accomplished by asking the question and then gathering information through phenomenological interviews and the literature review. Task two, the interpretive task, which focuses on analysis, was accomplished in chapter 4 by interpreting the data retrieved in the phenomenological interviews. The transcribed interviews were analyzed phenomenologically so that the essences of the

---

1. Ward, *Introducing Practical Theology*, 95.

trauma might come to the foreground; this garnered seven main essences discussed in detail in chapter 4.

The final two tasks of Osmer's approach are the ones utilized in this chapter and complete the practical theology interpretation. In task three, the normative task brings into conversation theological concepts so that we can "interpret particular episodes, situations, or contexts, constructing ethical norms to guide our responses."[2] Using the third task allows us to bring theology to the forefront. This task will allow an examination of the existing Pentecostal theology that contributes to Pentecostal triumphalism. Though some aspects of this triumphalism can lead to error, especially regarding suffering, as will be shown, there are also positive aspects that the Pentecostal theological locus provides. For example, the belief in the soon-coming King impels Pentecostals to live a lifestyle that actively fulfills the Great Commission. In addition, the belief in the miraculous provides hope during suffering, while this belief can also sometimes cause error when blame is tallied on the sufferer when the afflicted does not see relief.

Osmer's third task also allows us to explore the deficiencies of Pentecostal theology in light of trauma and suffering and to utilize Pentecostal scholarship, which has already identified problem areas, to suggest corrective measures. The issue at hand is not to deny existing Pentecostal theology but to add to what is there by having a more realistic view of suffering and how Pentecostals who suffer can experience God. A realistic view of suffering and experiencing God comes to the foreground in the third section of this chapter through examination of Luther's theology of the cross. Through contrast and comparison of Luther's *theologia crucis* with Pentecostal theology, the shortfalls of the Pentecostal theology in light of suffering will become apparent as will the usefulness of the inclusions of some of Luther's *theologia crucis* for Pentecostals who are enduring trauma and hardship.

Osmer's fourth task, the pragmatic task, allows for the determination of "strategies of action that will influence situations in ways that are desirable and entering into a reflective conversation with the 'talk back' emerging when they are enacted."[3] With the other three tasks completed, the fourth task utilizes the information garnered from them, and praxis is developed or suggested so that Pentecostal clergy and laity have an avenue to cope with trauma using spiritual tools. Luther's *theologia crucis* will allow for a deeper understanding of the presence of Christ during suffering,

---

2. Osmer, *Practical Theology*, 4.
3. Osmer, *Practical Theology*, 4.

even if the sufferer has no relief from suffering. It addresses the problem many Pentecostals encounter when unrequited suffering comes in conflict with an ideology that if they pray enough, God will make it all better. Additionally, Luther, through his *theologia crucis*, allows the sufferer to incorporate the practice of lament, this is explored further as an additive to Pentecostal praxis.

THE NORMATIVE TASK—WHAT SHOULD BE GOING ON?

Clergy often declared that there was no avenue for them to turn to spiritually when they were in the throes of trauma. During the interview process, Andrew exclaimed, "I think there is not a lot of room for these dark nights of the soul, and you know room for suffering because we're always looking for miraculous intervention." That candid response from Andrew reveals a theological mindset in Pentecostalism that does not readily accept suffering as an avenue to encounter God but instead looks for victory over the suffering. In his interview, Kirk shared a similar insight: "I don't like how in Pentecostal circles, in churches, we're not allowed to suffer. We're not allowed to share that we're suffering. We're not allowed to acknowledge it at all." The following section examines the existing Pentecostal theology that causes them to feel this way. The section after that will investigate Pentecostal scholarship, which has also identified problems in this area. The final section of the normative task will address Lutheran theology of the cross and discuss its implementation into Pentecostalism.

Pentecostal Triumphalism

The statements by both Andrew and Kirk reveal that their freedom to admit they are suffering as Pentecostal clergy is limited. Danny, in his interview, describes this situation as "I have a life of pain and what is pain? Like? It's kind of, you know, it's abstract at times. But I was raised in the Pentecostal church where you're supposed to live in victory all the time." David Courey suggests that early Pentecostalism "arose to challenge the triumphalism of complacent churches, but perhaps in spite of itself, developed its own form of triumphalism."[4] Courey's position is that Pentecostalism matured into a successful form of Evangelicalism which made

---

4. Courey, *What Has Wittenberg*, 16.

it a useful adaptation of evangelical piety, but in doing so "created its own crisis of expectation and experience."[5] There are three leading causes for this idea: the idea that we have power over evil, the idea of prosperity, and the eschatological view of immanence. The first two are rooted in the Pentecostal Christological lens, which declares Jesus as healer, and the third is linked to Jesus as soon coming King.[6] The first two items are highlighted in the interview with Will, who shared that he believed spiritual attacks were coming, but he was unsure what to do when there was no respite from the attacks; he shares that as a Pentecostal, "we're not, we don't share the struggles. We just want to share the victories and the numbers." Will's comment was not uncommon; others echoed it in the interview group who believed that Pentecostal praxis only allows for victory when facing an attack or suffering that persists.

Andrew, one of the interview participants, shared that he believed there was no room for embracing suffering because we always seek divine intervention to deliver us from the trying times. He believes it is a position that "does not stand up to the test of reality." Andrew's initial idea of divine intervention is what James Kwateng-Yeboah discusses when confronting triumphalism, "Importantly, the Pentecostalist power-over-evil theology fosters a dualistic cosmology of God and Satan as interpretive frameworks for good and evil in the physical world, a basis for theological ideals of prosperity as spiritual triumph over evil."[7] The dualistic cosmology of Pentecostals is similar to that which Luther himself held; Obermann says of him, "Christ and the Devil were equally real to him: one was the perpetual intercessor for Christianity, the other a menace to mankind till the end."[8] Luther, similar to Pentecostals, held to the concept that Christ was involved in a battle for the world; Pentecostals hold to an ideal of escapism that Christ would deliver them from this fight, while Luther's idea was that the fight was inescapable. According to Obermann, Luther believed Christ and Satan were in a cosmic struggle for control over the church and the world, and no one could avoid involvement in that struggle. Therefore, Christians

---

5. Courey, *What Has Wittenberg*, 17.

6. As stated earlier in the research, part of the Pentecostal Christology of the PAOC and PAONL declares four fundamental aspects concerning Christ, known as the *Full Gospel*. They are—Jesus is Savior, Jesus is Healer, Jesus is Baptiser in the Holy Spirit, Jesus is Soon Coming King. There are other streams of Pentecostalism which would add a fifth aspect which would be Jesus is Sanctifier.

7. Kwateng-Yeboah, "Poverty," 181.

8. Oberman, *Luther*, 104.

need the proper tools to survive this battle.[9] Pentecostals, on the other hand, believe they are endued with the power to counter the spiritual attacks of Satan. They believe this empowerment removes the power of the Devil over them. The interviews revealed that Mark tried multiple spiritual methods to try and relieve his affliction to see if they would work to give him relief from the effects of trauma, "I would pick and choose to see what would work" he says. In doing this, he was seeking a quick cure for the effects of his traumatic situation, even though that cure never came quickly. Luther's view on this subject allows continued suffering to occur to the Christ follower but allows for experiencing a deeper sense of Christ in our suffering. If Mark and other Pentecostals had incorporated a more Lutheran ideal of suffering into their praxis and theology, there would have been far fewer moments of crisis of faith during suffering.

The Pentecostal view of power over the enemy has some validity, but it is often overstated, leading them to ignore personal suffering that may occur outside of the spiritual realm and instead declare that they are due to the enemy. They often believe that the sufferer must have erred if a person is under persistent affliction. For many participants, this was a familiar cry during the phenomenological interviews. Connie, for example, describes it this way, "And it made me question my life, how much God loved me because, again, I kind of caught myself defaulting to that. Everything that I loved was based on works, or I must have done something wrong." Jackie, meanwhile, describes it as a "warped sense of personal responsibility." These responses by Connie and Jackie were not unique; others shared feelings that made them accept personal responsibility for their affliction, from not having enough faith to not praying enough. Connie and Jackie seek escape and put the blame of continued suffering on their lack of proper works, an entirely non-Lutheran and non-Pentecostal theological position. However, what is an official doctrine in Pentecostalism, and what the actual praxis is, sometimes differ. If Pentecostals were to acknowledge our helplessness in the face of suffering and seek the presence of Christ, there would be the benefit of coming into a deeper understanding of Christ and His suffering.

While not official doctrine, the trend of placing blame on themselves or Satan is apparent from the beginning of the Pentecostal movement. The works of Frank Bartleman, the early Pentecostal biographer who writes about his meetings in the early days of the Pentecostal movement, offer a glimpse of this, "We went on to Elkland, nearby. Here we had a great battle.

9. Oberman, *Luther*, 104.

A child had a whining demon, and a dog seemed possessed with barking. This disturbed the meetings greatly. I spoke four times at the latter place and many received help and blessing."[10] The whining baby and the barking dog were attributed to demonic works, but Bartleman's last sentence in that quote shows that even despite what he viewed as demonic, he still had victory because many received help and blessings. Although Bartleman was an American, the same fundamental unofficial theology was at work on the Canadian side of the border. In a letter dated February 15, 1954, by Essie Watson, the wife of PAOC church planter and evangelist Raymond Watson, she describes their ministry from the 1920s until 1930 in Canada. Recalling their work in St. Thomas, Ontario, she says, "we moved to a hall—a dance hall, and a lovely one. Well, the devil was there, but was routed by the power of God and prayer. So much that when they had their annual Police-mans Ball—this had always been a big event. Do you know how many couples turned out?—Five, and THEY COULDN'T DANCE."[11] Bartleman and Watson's accounts highlight that the early Pentecostals emphasize victory over Satan when facing adversity, but their accounts are just a sample of the much larger body of early Pentecostal works which incorporate the battle and victory framework.[12] Pentecostals view the miraculous as a breaking in of the Kingdom of God so that their message would have power. They use the miraculous as a sign that God is at work in their lives, and when the miracles fail to happen, they may start to doubt God's presence with them.[13] While most modern Pentecostals do not believe that the devil is responsible for every adversity, there are still the underpinnings of that belief. In his essay in *Pentecostal Gifts and Ministries in a Postmodern Era*, Christopher Gornold-Smith writes,

---

10. Bartleman, *How Pentecost Came*, 118.

11. Watson, Essie. *Essie Watson to Walter McAlister*, February 15, 1954, PAOC National Archives.

12. Qualls, *God Forgive Us*, 85. Qualls provides another story from the early days of the modern Pentecostal movement where the victory over the demonic narrative was at work. Corum and Amanda Benedict had travelled to St. Louis, MS to hold meetings. While there they felt that there were demonic forces at work, the solution of Amanda Benedict was, "For a year, she ate nothing but bread and water, and she stayed in the tent erected for the Pentecostal meetings to pray for victory over these dark powers."

13. Pentecostals will use passages such as Luke 7:18–2, Acts 1:8, Acts 2 or a variety of other scriptures to establish that their message receives importance when it is accompanied by the miraculous.

> The need to perceive what is going on in the spiritual realm is not a theoretical problem and is not confined to church meetings. . . . An inner witness from the Holy Spirit can guide the Christian believer. Such a witness can only be described as an irresistible and profound conviction that one is in the presence of something intensely evil and more than human.[14]

Gornold-Smith shows that Pentecostals still have a propensity to view things from a lens of spiritual warfare, which can cause people in suffering to view it as an attack of the enemy when it may be happening for other reasons. That is not to say that Pentecostals should discard the spiritual warfare framework; instead, they should develop the concept more fully but allow for nuance so that suffering people will not feel guilty or ashamed when they do not find the relief they are seeking in prayer.

The second cause of this idea of Pentecostal triumphalism is rooted in the concept of prosperity. Even if the prosperity to which Pentecostals adhere is not an extreme version, such as those from fringe Pentecostals like Kenneth Hagin, Kenneth Copeland, or others, it leads to beliefs that can cause Pentecostal clergy to see victory and spiritual triumph as their Christian privilege. Jesus is healer, as discussed in chapter 2, is one of the fourfold views of Christ held by the PAOC and PAONL. That doctrine comes with the idea of a physical and holistic view of healing. Frank Macchia links the doctrine of healing with a predisposition to a prosperity belief.

> The healing doctrine also reveals the somewhat "material" understanding of salvation among Pentecostals. Salvation is not only of the soul but also for general well being in this life. This assumption is widespread among Pentecostals today globally, leading increasing numbers toward an exaggerated "health and wealth" gospel that promises prosperity and good health to all of the redeemed. Though this trend seems extreme to many, it is rooted in an impulse that is quite distinctively Pentecostal.[15]

Macchia shows that exaggerated teachings on prosperity and health are a leading factor in holding to a view of triumph in all aspects of life. Pentecostals would instead focus on the concepts that suggest victory is at hand rather than struggle with life's realities. Craig Keener notes that Pentecostals would rather have; "Teachings on generational curses, prosperity, and, in various ways, controlling our own destinies have often proved more

---

14. Gornold-Smith, "Spiritual Gifts," 33.
15. Macchia, *Baptized*, 17.

appealing in our consumer culture than training for personal evangelism, trusting God during hardship, or reading Scripture in context."[16] Keener's point is that Pentecostals want to have methods to control their destinies, so they turn to a myriad of spiritual solutions to enable that. If a problem arises, we can pray that away or utilize another method to achieve our desired results. The idea of spiritual experimentation was brought up in the interview with Mark, who said he noticed in the Bible that the characters

> didn't ask God; they just declared it. And we see both kinds in scripture, those petitions, but also those prayers of faith; we already know what God's will is. And you just declare it. And I found myself trying all those. Almost like I'm just picking and choosing to see what'll work. And so there was a little bit of experimenting.

Mark's praxis during trauma was a representation of what Keener describes above. However, Mark's response was not rooted in trauma but in his theological background that seeks victory and triumph. It would seem that Mark's response is akin to that which Courey posits is "Faith placed in slogans, formulae and verses brings the reductionist nature of Pentecostal triumphalism most clearly into focus. The populist appeal of Pentecostalism lends itself to simplistic solutions to multifaceted issues."[17] Jackie, on the other hand, declared that her traumatic experience caused her to "appreciate that life is not fair and we are not guaranteed the prosperity version of the gospel." Her trauma brought about a new perspective which is not typically Pentecostal, but instead allows for faithful service to God even when life is not perfect.

The non-Pentecostal almost always assumes that the heart of Pentecostal theology is centred around Spirit baptism; that is not the case. According to Macchia, the defining theology is eschatology, which has the idea that the kingdom of God has broken into this present world, and Pentecostal believers are living in an already but not yet state of the kingdom of God being established. Macchia writes, "Interestingly, it is not Spirit baptism but eschatology (especially in relation to a passion for mission) that has been most used among Pentecostal theologians of recent to achieve coherence for that which is distinctive about Pentecostal theology."[18] Pentecostals

---

16. Keener, *Spirit Hermeneutics*, 276.
17. Courey, *What Has Wittenberg*, 8.
18. Macchia, *Baptized*, 25. Macchia also warns on page 161 of this work that there are two extremes to avoid when comparing the Kingdom or Christ to the church. The first is a separation or a dualism, and the second is an identification between Christ or His

historically have viewed themselves in the last of the last days. While this has softened somewhat, Pentecostals still consider themselves an end-time movement. This view affects the Pentecostal's worship, witness, and praxis, all of which, if taken to an extreme, can lead to a sense of exceptionalism and triumphalism. Telford Work writes in *The Oxford History of Christian Worship* concerning Pentecostals,

> Worshipers experience the eschatological presence of God and God's cloud of witnesses as the Spirit fuses temporal and spatial horizons. God's presence transforms a primitive storefront church sanctuary into the heavenly throne room into which the nations are gathered and from which prophets and apostles are sent to proclaim the good news.[19]

Pentecostals come into their worship service expecting the Divine to break through and that a sense of the eschatological kingdom will be present; this can prove problematic when you expect God's presence to be felt but feel that He has abandoned you, or that you are unworthy of Him. Jason's conundrum typifies this issue, he wanted to experience the presence of God but said, "I just had this silly idea that God had abandoned me, that he had given up on me and that I wasn't even a fit to, to go into his presence." This end-time view of the Pentecostals can also lead to a sense of triumphalism, with the belief that Christ is coming soon being a predominant theological belief among PAOC and PAONL clergy; it promulgates within them the concept that their Christian calling to be one of end-time significance. Byron D. Klaus posits that this "sense of participation in a story of eschatological significance, supported by supernatural Spirit empowerment(s), creates a strong sense of destiny in the Pentecostal identity. Only the divine intrusion of the Spirit of God is viewed as an adequate eternal resource for the end-time harvest."[20] Pentecostals believe it is their destiny to be a part of the end-time mission of God; if God had called them into this task, then surely nothing would stop them. Therefore, the Pentecostal ethos is summarized best by Klaus, "The existence of this newly created 'eschatological community' was centred in their reliance on the Spirit's empowerment to bear witness, in word, deed, and power that the reality of the kingdom of

---

kingdom and the church, which can lead to an over-realized eschatology and the loss of a proper emphasis on the church during renewal as a servant to Christ.

19. Work, "Pentecostal and Charismatic Worship," 578.
20. Klaus, "Implications," 131.

God was visible among them."[21] Pentecostals see the giftings of the Spirit as a sign that the eschatological kingdom is, in part, breaking into the present world. I do not suggest removing the eschatological view or altering them in theory. However, their practical application should be adjusted so that when in the face of trouble, Pentecostals do not doubt their theology, but they can realize that, theologically speaking, there are many facets to the human experience. In discussing the eschatological framework which Pentecostals hold, Andrew shares the opinion that the escapist theology of Pentecostals, that Jesus will remove us from this present trouble also infiltrates daily church life; suggesting that this causes the people to only want "the positive answer" to the questions of how people are doing. When victory is not granted or is a long way off, we need to view our experience not as a defeat but as an opportunity to grow in Christ, yet this is rarely if ever done in Pentecostalism. Some Pentecostals have suggested that we would be better served if we considered Spirit baptism in the enduement of power for being a witness and to give it the fuller meaning of baptism into divine love, "the greatest release of the Spirit is in the form of divine love, to which all these gifts point and from which they draw their strength as pointers to the power of the kingdom of God to transform lives."[22] With divine love as the motivating force, it can allow the Pentecostal believer not to see things in terms of victory; but instead, Spirit baptism is viewed as the presence of God manifest to us in His love, where we take part in the *perichoretic* dance of the Trinity.[23] Viewing the Spirit baptism as an act of divine love will allow the Pentecostal to understand that the Christian life is not one of constant victory as we traverse our earthly existence; instead, it points to the cross as the point of triumph in suffering. Jackie believes that Pentecostals have not considered the depths of benefit from their suffering. She says Pentecostals "have failed to consider suffering and the beautiful things that can come out of suffering and the way that God meets us there, you know, and, and we have presented this very unrealistic and way that we think God moves among us or he guarantees us or promises us." These "beautiful things" as Jackie aptly declares them allows the presence of Christ to become manifest during the darkest times of the sufferer, it allows them to cry out to God asking where He is, and in turn expect an answer from Him akin to the

---

21. Klaus, "Implications," 137.
22. Macchia, *Baptized*, 127.
23. Macchia, *Baptized*, 223.

authors of the Psalms of lament, this is viewing the cross as triumph despite suffering.

The cross as triumph amidst suffering is what Ivan Satyavarata refers to as a paradox, which reminds us "that while Christian triumph is inevitable, it is a triumph centered in death and servanthood. We thus need not recoil from a triumphalism that is rooted in the self-giving love of God as revealed in Christ crucified, which seeks to advance the kingdom mission of God in humble dependence on God's Spirit."[24]

No one wants to remain in a tragic situation where suffering abounds, so it is natural that Pentecostals seek to alleviate their suffering. In their desire to be free of negative experience, they either deny its existence, accredit it to malevolent forces, or simply declare it is not God's will. In His moment of suffering, Christ prayed for the cross to be taken away, yet he acquiesced to the will of the Father. This research does not suggest that Pentecostals remove the doctrines of healing, prosperity, or even their eschatology. Instead, I suggest that Pentecostals develop a refined view of those doctrines that do not hold to a universalistic view of triumph but allow for a more realistic view of suffering when relief does not come. The danger of not enacting a more holistic approach to suffering and trauma lies in the idea that there can be a tendency to pull away from God without a theological scope from which to draw. Pulling away from God happened in many phenomenological interviews where the subjects felt God abandoned them, so they, in turn, pulled away from Him. Connie's interview provides a clear example of this, "I started recognizing that I was in a numbing relationship with God, or I just felt like I was going through the motions as opposed to depth." The lack of an outlet, imposed by Pentecostal triumphalism, led her to a spiritual numbness in her relationship with Christ.

Pentecostals want to see the Spirit at work in their lives through supernatural manifestations; these are seen as a foretaste of the kingdom to come. Yes, they hope for the future, but impatience is at their core, and they want blessings now. In *Pentecostal Spirituality: A Passion for the Kingdom*, Steven Jack Land writes that for Pentecostals, the starting point "is the Holy Spirit who is 'God with us.' The God who was present among Israel and in Jesus Christ is now present as the Holy Spirit. The God who will one day be 'all in all' is at work now in all things, working together for the good of those who love Him."[25] Land's point is that in Pentecostal spirituality, the

24. Satyavarata, "Friends in Mission," 218.
25. Land, *Pentecostal Spirituality*, 21.

idea is that there is a promise of victory in the earthly mission of the Pentecostal. Land believes Pentecostals affirm along with Barth that "Prayer is an eschatological cry based on acknowledgement of logical reality that is possible here and there."[26] While Barth and the Pentecostals are correct in their assumptions that there is the possibility of victory here and assurance of victory there (heaven), Pentecostals often forget that there is also the possibility of suffering here while having victory there. Land suggests that the Pentecostals saw themselves not as wandering in the wilderness but as living in the Promised Land. They were no longer in the Temple's outer courts but were now in the inner sanctum of the Holy of Holies.[27] The idea that Pentecostals were in the inner sanctum through the Spirit was a significant outlook of the initial Pentecostals but has also remained a prevalent outlook among modern Pentecostals as well. Spiritually they see themselves in the final destination, the inner sanctum or the Promised Land. They are in the places of promise, no longer facing hardships. Instead, they are in the places where the glory was residing; the *already but not yet* mentality they hold to has made them susceptible to believing that no bad thing should happen because they were living in God's promises. While they hold tremendous value in the cross for its salvific purposes, they do not see it as anything other than a place to have our sins forgiven. They do not identify with Christ's sufferings other than acknowledging that he took our punishment for us. Macchia declares tension exists in the "hidden meaning of faith and the visible signs by which faith reaches for the new creation to come."[28] He suggests that the tension should not be resolved by reducing faith to hidden meanings or visible triumphs over suffering. Faith can become passive if the former is done, providing no immediate hope for those suffering. If the latter is done, then a person's faith can become triumphalistic with no meaningful way to comfort those who live in a state of suffering. David Courey postulates that despite Pentecostalism's success that there is within it an inherent conflict, "The Pentecostal narrative suggests that once one has experienced true salvation, and fullness of the Spirit, the result should be the 'victorious Christian life.'"[29]

    Pentecostals have erred on the side of expecting God to move if certain conditions are met, if we pray enough, are holy enough, give enough

26. Land, *Pentecostal Spirituality*, 25.
27. Land, *Pentecostal Spirituality*, 67.
28. Macchia, *Baptized*, 125.
29. Courey, *What Has Wittenberg*, 3.

to the church, and the list could go on. We have minimalized our faith and the working of miracles to some formulaic steps that supposedly ensure victory.[30] Connie's interview describes this very issue well; on multiple occasions, she wondered what she did to cause her suffering or what she could do to alleviate it. Torr says that Pentecostals and Charismatics have an imbalance in how they respond to "suffering which appears innocent and meaningless and in which God seems somehow absent."[31] This imbalance can be attributed to the Pentecostals' lacuna regarding suffering. Martin Mittelstadt's work *The Spirit and Suffering in Luke-Acts* discusses this gap and says that in the Pentecostal efforts to defend their distinctive baptism in the Holy Spirit, that other pneumatological emphasis of Luke are overlooked. Namely that, "the Pentecostal tradition, at a scholarly and experiential level, has generally neglected to address and apply the role of the Holy Spirit in contexts of suffering and persecution."[32] Mittelstadt encourages his readers to read Luke's works with an eye on the sustaining work of the Holy Spirit through times of suffering, understanding that while suffering may persist, the Holy Spirit is with the believer in their suffering.[33] Another Pentecostal theologian, Kärkkäinen declares that the problem for Pentecostals is that they do not know what to do when the negative side of the Christian life happens, which leads them to have few options;

> disappointments when the healing did not come, agony when one faces the death of a loved one despite prayers of faith, the tragedy of financial breakdown, and so on. In fact, many Pentecostals and charismatics have been left with few options: either to deny experiences that seem to shatter one's faith, to blame oneself or other persons involved for the lack of faith, or to give up one's faith.[34]

Kärkkäinen proposes that Pentecostals and charismatics do not neglect to talk about faith, power, healing and miracles. However, they must also ensure they are adequately equipped to handle the times when facing topics such as "the existence of suffering, the duality of human faith, the

---

30. Keener, *Spirit Hermeneutics*, 28. Keener argues that sometimes because Pentecostals view God as active it has led to reductionism in faith. The believer believes that if certain steps are taken then their prayers will be answered.

31. Torr, *Dramatic*, 2.

32. Mittelstadt, *The Spirit and Suffering*, 3.

33. Mittelstadt, *The Spirit and Suffering*, 8–9.

34. Kärkkäinen, "Theology of the Cross," 151.

mystery of God's hiddenness, and the ultimate fate of everyone, death."[35] However, Kärkkäinen's suggestion to admit suffering is foreign to Pentecostals. Mark posited this when he stated, "But if you're in a church and a, like a typical traditional Pentecostal church, and you would share something like I'm feeling bad or something, it's like, they tell you not to speak that. Don't speak that truth, this name, it, claim it. Just say that you're okay. And you're going to be okay. I hate that stuff." Pamela F. Engelbert, a Pentecostal, examines the experience of unanswered prayers in her book *Who Is Present in Absence?* During this examination, she uncovers that when the Pentecostal believer seeks divine intervention on a matter and is only met with silence, they are experiencing God's absence or hiddenness. Engelbert ascertains, "This means I am equating the experience of the lack of an expected divine intervention with God's apparent absence."[36] Luther also understood the hiddenness of God experienced in suffering and chose to believe in God's goodness despite the Creator's silence. Dennis Ngien shares regarding Luther that he "still believes in the goodness of God against the contrary appearances. The certainty of his faith lies with the incarnate God."[37] The goodness of God that Luther is sure of should be the attitude which the Pentecostal clergy person is also confident in even in the midst of suffering.

So then, how can Pentecostal theologians, pastors, and leaders solve this problem since Pentecostals have no system to comprehend their suffering in light of triumphalistic biases? The remedy is to make the central focus the cross for those in trauma, emphasizing not only the victory we receive at the cross but also the idea that we suffer with Christ at the cross. The concept of meeting Christ in suffering is a central aspect of Luther's *theologia crucis* and should be brought to the forefront for usage in Pentecostal theology.

The theologians presented thus far believe that Pentecostals need to utilize Luther's theology as a conversation partner to grasp better the reality of suffering during trauma. Kärkkäinen opines that Pentecostal Christians and theologians need something to help them face the darker points in life. He says that Luther's theology of the cross will help Pentecostals "to deal with the issues of suffering, disappointments, and failures."[38] Similarly, David Courey suggests that "Pentecostalism is at an impasse between

---

35. Kärkkäinen, "Theology of the Cross," 151.
36. Engelbert, *Who Is Present*, 29.
37. Ngien, *Fruit for the Soul*, 76.
38. Kärkkäinen, "Theology of the Cross," 152.

expectancy and experience that can be resolved through an application of Luther's theology of the cross, which will liberate it to continued development as a viable expression of Christianity in the twenty-first century."[39]

The phenomenological research highlighted that many participants did not feel that their existing theology or praxis was suitable when they suffered, and now the project explores Luther's *theologia crucis* so that a discussion may occur on how it might be integrated theologically with Pentecostal theology and praxis. The existing Pentecostal theology has much value; however, additions should be made which will temper some extremes, such as hyper faith, while allowing the sufferer to experience the grace of God during trials. These additions are something which David Courey promotes and believes the *theologia crucis* is not meant to be "a damning bludgeon with which to decimate the entire Pentecostal project as a *theologia gloria*. Instead, the cross may be seen as a constructive corrective that affirms some of the basic impulses of Pentecostalism."[40] The theology of the cross can offer correction to some of the more extreme positions within Pentecostalism without compromising the basics of Pentecostal theology.

Theologia Crucis for Pentecostals

The Pentecostal theological lens is focused on triumph, which the reformer Martin Luther would refer to as a theology of glory. Luther contrasts a theology of glory with a theology of the cross in *Heidelberg Disputation* theses twenty-one, "A theology of glory calls evil good and good evil. A theology of the cross calls the thing what it actually is. This is clear: He who does not know Christ does not know God hidden in suffering."[41] Luther sees value in embracing suffering so that the follower of Christ can see God through it. Gerhard Forde points out, "A theology of the cross, however, is not sentimentalism. To be sure, it speaks much about suffering. A theologian of the cross, Luther says, looks at all things through suffering and the cross. It is also certainly true that Christ in God enters into our suffering and death."[42] During his interview, Danny suggested that Pentecostals have no praxis which adequately accounts for moments of suffering; he states, "I have a life

---

39. Courey, *What Has Wittenberg*, 3.
40. Courey, *What Has Wittenberg*, 115.
41. Luther, "Heidelberg Disputation (1518)."
42. Forde and Luther, *On Being*, viii.

of pain, but I was raised in the Pentecostal church where you are supposed to have the victory all the time." Through this statement, he reveals that his Pentecostal theology and praxis come from a place of sentimentalism, but as he expounds on his thoughts, he shares that there needs to be a "balance, for you read in the scriptures that you will have tribulations. I know we have the victory, but sometimes life just sucks." This internal conflict between what is expected, the victory and the realities of life brings pain, which many who do not have a proper *theologia crucis* often struggle with. These people are often hindered in their spiritual development when suffering comes their way since their mindset of victory and triumphalism is predominantly sentimental in nature. For Luther, a theology of the cross is more than just simply sentimentally surveying that wonderous old cross; instead, he understands Christ entering into our suffering through what He did on the cross. To do what Luther suggests in disputation twenty-one and call the thing what it actually is, would mean that the theologian of the cross is not willing to trim their language as to "not to give offence, to stroke the psyche rather than place it under attack."[43] A theologian of the cross instead understands everything through the cross, and declares that there is no good in us. While suffering, the objective of the theologian of the cross is to see our unworthiness and embrace Christ, who suffers with us. However, according to Forde, the problem is that the theology of glory is persistent and never vanishes: "It is the perennial theology of the fallen race."[44] The theology of glory seeks to find ways to better the human race, to allow, through good works, access to God's presence. The sufferer who utilizes a theology of glory wonders what they can do to remedy their situation. Some interview participants displayed this type of understanding; for example, Mark shared that he experimented with many spiritual practices to see what would work to get him out of his traumatic situation. He said he "got to a place where he was trying to manipulate God through the practices." Other participants wondered if their trauma occurred to them because of something wrong they did, or perhaps they did not pray enough or read the Bible enough. A battle takes place in the mind of the Pentecostal believer, wondering if there is something they can do to earn more of God's blessing. The theology of the cross declares there is nothing we can do to earn blessing or favour, and instead, "the preacher-theologian must know

---

43. Forde and Luther, *On Being*, x.
44. Forde and Luther, *On Being*, xiii.

this and learn how to use the word of the cross in that combat."[45] The theologian of the cross faces the problems, joys, and sorrows in their daily lives instead of seeking to remove the negative parts from them. Forde uses the idea that the theologian of glory seeks escape hatches in their lives instead of confronting the suffering.[46] The theologian of glory seeks to remove their suffering. In doing so, "the theologian of glory and unbelievers tend to devise their own ladders to God. . .thereby bypassing the revealed God."[47] Luther believed God is perfectly revealed in the cross and in Christ's suffering. When the Christian seeks to escape their suffering, opting instead for a way of glory, they ignore the revealed God on the cross and instead fabricate an erroneous view of God.

Luther uses thesis three and four of the Heidelberg disputation to highlight the futility of the works of man compared to the works of God. In thesis three, Luther describes the human works which seem "attractive and good, they are nevertheless likely to be mortal sins."[48] In contrast, he states that the works of God are "always unattractive and appear evil"[49] but are the only works which have merit. Luther describes a works-based theology of glory as having no value in these two theses. Officially, the PAOC and PAONL are not works-based; however, the interviews reveal that there are some underpinnings of that conceptual framework. When interviewed, Jackie says, "I deserved bad things," and she offers a work-based ideal. Connie shared that she believed God would keep her trauma away if she read her bible enough or engaged in spiritual practices. Their accounts give credence to the criticism of Thomas Smail against the Pentecostal and Charismatic movements who said their theology "springs from a *theologia gloriae* that does not wrestle with a *theologia crucis* and so concentrates too one-sidedly on the triumphs of Easter and Pentecost and does not sufficiently take into account that they can only be reached by way of the cross."[50] The mindset of those who believe they can get more incredible blessings by doing more significant works for God is spoken of derisively by Luther, "A theologian of glory calls suffering evil while he calls works good. In fact, he works to

---

45. Forde and Luther, *On Being*, 4.
46. Forde and Luther, *On Being*, 15.
47. Ngien, *Fruit for the Soul*, 74–75.
48. Luther, "Heidelberg Disputation (1518)."
49. Luther, "Heidelberg Disputation (1518)."
50. Smail, "Cross and the Spirit," 15.

avoid suffering. And if he is afflicted with adversity, he concludes that he failed in his works."[51]

Luther also posits in thesis twenty, "But he is worthy to be called a theologian who looks at the hidden things and "backside" of God (*posteriori Dei*) [Exodus 33:23] as being seen through sufferings and the cross."[52] In his proofs for this thesis, Luther declares that those things which are the backside of God are the things "The Apostle in 1 Cor. 1:25 calls them the weakness and folly of God. Because men misused the knowledge of God through works, God wished again to be recognized in suffering, and to condemn wisdom concerning invisible things."[53] The theologian of glory seeks revelation outside of the cross in their works, whereas the theologian of the cross seeks to know Christ in suffering. This concept of Luther is of significance in this study, for Pentecostals must not seek to know God by escaping their trauma and suffering but instead should look at the backside of God and embrace the suffering as Christ embraces us in it. Kirk suggested during his interview that Pentecostals would be wise if they embraced suffering as something where Christ can draw near and we can experience Christ's presence during our suffering and that it should also provide an opportunity for "suffering together as the body at the cross." Kirk's concept is that we need to move the church from where only victorious moments are shared to where the church mourns with the mourner and suffers with the sufferer. As a community, they find solace in Christ and His suffering with us, where we move from an ideal of glory only to a place where hurt brings us into the presence of God in just as meaningful a way as hope does.

Luther saw the danger of only looking at the glory of our relationship with Christ. He realized that we could only know Christ fully when we broach the uncomfortable topics and realize that we can embrace our suffering at the cross. In encouraging Pentecostals to embrace more of a theology of the cross, Courey states, "Not only is Christ's cross the place of divine hiddenness, but our own cross becomes the place of divine revelation."[54] Adding this theological concept to Pentecostalism will help them to understand a more holistic view of the Christian concept of suffering. Expansion of their views of suffering will help them develop strategies and spiritual

---

51. Luther, "Heidelberg Disputation (1518)."
52. Luther, "Heidelberg Disputation (1518)."
53. Luther, "Heidelberg Disputation (1518)."
54. Courey, *What Has Wittenberg*, 166.

practices to cope while enduring persistent trauma and allow us to experience God during it.

Richard Eyer, who penned the book *Pastoral Care Under the Cross*, provides insight into the Lutheran perspective of suffering, "The posture of kneeling at the foot of the cross enables us to see God at work in suffering. Ironically, our helplessness makes it possible to see God. This is true not only for the suffering parishioner but also for the pastor who suffers with the suffering parishioner."[55] Eyer believes that it is at the foot of the cross where we discover the meaning of the cross, and that defeat is the way of the cross where when acknowledged through faith, it becomes our victory. Pentecostals would be well served to re-examine their theology by adding Luther's *theologia crucis*; this is not a call to a pessimistic faith but rather a faith that is well-rounded and understands that in our suffering, there is an opportunity to identify with the suffering of Christ on the cross. So that we can vocalize our anguish honestly before God just as Christ did on the cross when he proclaimed, "God, why have you forsaken me?" This idea of honest vocalization will be expanded further in the coming pages as we explore Osmer's pragmatic task. Many of this study's phenomenological participants empathized with Christ's cry; they proclaimed that they experienced God's hiddenness or His seeming lack of care. Since their theology and praxis do not currently have adequate response methods, they often did not know what to do. I suggest the following: first is the utilization of Luther's *theologia crucis* in Pentecostal theology, and then utilizing that theology into a Luther-inspired practice of lament.

THE PRAGMATIC TASK—HOW MIGHT WE RESPOND?

As has already been ascertained, North American Pentecostal churches have long lived with a sense of exceptionalism and triumphalism, which is not solely a church issue but rampant in North American society, where there is an ideal that declares, "we are the best." As this mindset has crept into the North American church, it has also affected the congregant's relationship with God. They have a problem expressing themselves to the Almighty unless it is in joy or penitence; however, that penitence is only used to move them immediately back to a place of joy. In contrast, the range of emotions expressed through the Psalms is quite different than what is allowed in Pentecostal spirituality; in the Psalms, there are cries of distress,

---

55. Eyer, *Pastoral Care*, 33.

abandonment, sorrow, joy, hope, and all the range of human emotion. The Psalmists may feel abandoned, and so they utter phrases like "How long, O Lord? Will you forget me forever?" (Ps. 13:1a ESV) They do not hold back their anger towards God while suffering, so they hurl accusatory cries toward God in what seems to be their darkest moments. Psalm 42 highlights an interaction like this; the writer states a desire for God to draw close to them while they accuse the Almighty of forgetting them (Psalm 42:9). Psalm 42 does not speak of wanting more of God because they are already experiencing His goodness; it is a Psalm that says they need Him because there is this overwhelming sense of abandonment that they are experiencing. While accusing God may not be something we are accustomed to, Elizabeth Liebert condones the practice of crying out against God and deems it as an "implicit act of faith."[56]

Luther likewise utilizes the Psalms of lament as a source of praxis for his spirituality. Ngien states that the "proper usage of God's word, with the lament Psalms in view, as a method of comfort is integral to Luther's pastoral call."[57] Luther saw value in lament and utilized it in his own Christian life, he believed that the Psalms contained the fullness of the gospel message and valued them more than any other book of the Bible, referring to them as "a little Bible."[58] Luther's theology of the cross and his interpretation of the Bible, especially the Psalms, were intrinsically linked. What he laid out in his Heidelberg Disputation would "continue to govern his interpretation of the Psalms."[59] If being a theologian of the cross is to call a thing what it actually is, then a theologian of the cross "voices complaints as they actually are and speaks earnestly from the bottom of the heart to God with an unmitigated effrontery, devoid of pretense and avoidance. Above all, only a true theologian of the cross hears God speaking in his affliction, even contrary to his expectations and in God's apparent absence."[60]

Cries to God when joy is absent remind us that we are entirely reliant on God. Jason shared that while he was in the throes of his traumatic reaction, he was inexplicably drawn to the Book of Lamentations in the Bible:

> The silly thing is, is I kept on going to the book of Lamentations as I'm going through, that's what I'm reading. That's what I'm

56. Liebert, *Soul of Discernment*, 94.
57. Ngien, *Fruit for the Soul*, xxv.
58. Ngien, *Fruit for the Soul*, xviii.
59. Ngien, *Fruit for the Soul*, xxiv.
60. Ngien, *Fruit for the Soul*, xxix.

studying. Like why, right? Why am I going to the book of Lamentations? But I wanted something to relate, something that related to kind of what I was going through, I guess, Lamentations with kind of a downer book. There's not a whole lot of rejoicing in that book. And that that's kind of where, where I was at.

It was during his trauma that Jason felt a need to understand what he was encountering in his own spiritual walk by reading the account of Jeremiah in Lamentations. Moreover, in Lamentations and the Psalms of Lament, the readers can encounter a level of honesty with God that may seem sacrilegious to some. The question must be raised for the person not accustomed to utilizing lament and may feel guilty, is there a difference in its appropriateness if we already think those thoughts? Does he not all ready know how we feel? Some may express what others deem inappropriate accusations against the Almighty, but if the accusations are viewed in light of the Psalms of Lament, it will be seen that they are a scriptural practice. Therefore, the cries of our souls must be entrenched in our faith in God. We cry out only because we know He is the only one who can answer our cries. A person lamenting will either fall into despair and blame God or allow their situation to move them towards God; this is why it is necessary to have a proper view of lament and suffering and utilizing the theology of the cross will aid in this. Luther did not view lamentation as a sin or blasphemy; instead, he was "far from rejecting lamentation as an unwitting sin of blasphemy of suppressing it as an irrational act, Luther asserted that the whole of the believer's life is lamentation, genuine and godly."[61] Luther saw that controlled lamentation was not only permissible but beneficial for the believer and rightfully belonged to what Luther referred to as a theology of the cross. According to Ngien, Luther had deemed that lamentation was appropriate:

> in times of pain and desolation. Namely, there is a place in theology and liturgy for genuine lamentation that stems from a pure heart, disposed to repose in God's unfailing love, even at times of desolation and grief. However, one must exercise faith and moderation in the expression of lament, which not only protects the faithful from degenerating into sin and rebellion against God.[62]

Ngien rightly points out that believers must guard themselves when using lament and utilize both moderation and faith when in the process of

---

61. Ngien, *Fruit for the Soul*, 2.
62. Ngien, *Fruit for the Soul*, xxvi.

lament. The difference between godly and sinful lament can be understood through understanding the difference of how suffering is understood in a *theologia crucis* versus a *theologia gloriae*. The theologian of glory does not acknowledge that the suffering may be sent by God or at minimum used by God, whereas the theologian of the cross accepts "that they are sent by God and are not without purpose."[63] Whereas the theologian of the cross understands that suffering may be brought on them by God, and even if it is not, it is still a place to meet Christ in our suffering.

In modern psychotherapeutics, remembering and relaying the painful moments is considered processing a problematic reaction point (PRP).[64] Recalling the reaction point allows the complainant to understand where their emotions have prompted them to overreact. They then understand the stimulus for the reaction that caused them to act/react. After that, they understand that action/reaction may include behaviours or feelings or possibly both. Finally, the person comes to understand their reaction as being problematic.[65] If we use these three areas to examine our lament, we will begin to better understand the emotional baggage we have with God.

These three aspects are seen in many of the Psalms of Lament using a PRP methodology. Psalm 74, for example, contains all of these aspects. The reaction is to call out to God in an accusatory tone, and we find the stimulus for that reaction, as shown in verses 1–11. God has forgotten them, and the enemy is hounding them. The second step of the PRP is also found in the first few verses of the Psalm; they ask God why they are "cast off forever" and continue with a plea for God to remember them again. In that Psalm, we see raw emotion, no holding back, and open and transparent communication to God. It is not emotion couched in gracefulness; it is the cry of an anguished heart. Finally, the psalmist sees that the reaction is problematic, an overreaction and remembers the faithfulness of God instead. The examination of their PRP allows them to see that there is an issue with remaining accusatory, and instead, we must move to trust God. A person who is angry at God and never examines their motives will invariably abandon a relationship with God.

Strangely, our society is willing to vent to psychotherapists, politicians, doctors, pastors, and the grocery clerk that bags your groceries, but we are unwilling to vent at God. Perhaps because we view it as a negative emotion

---

63. Ngien, *Fruit for the Soul*, 4.
64. Patton, *From Ministry*, 31.
65. Patton, *From Ministry*, 31.

or we do not want to disrespect God, but is our being less than honest with God going to enhance our spiritual walk? While the PRP concept may not translate perfectly to the Psalms, it reveals that emotions and reactions to suffering are normative behaviour in these messy lives.

Our world is not one where everyone lives "happily ever after"; instead, there is a constant cycle between the extremes of joy and pain. It is in the joy that people are in a state of equilibrium. However, the moments of pain thrust people into disequilibrium; during those moments, they cry out in anguish. The Psalms of Lament reveal that the psalmist is in a state of disequilibrium. Then, the psalmists realize that "life is not as it should be, and in these psalms, the psalmists lament, protest, and call God to account."[66] To relearn to capture the ability to lament before God, to cry out when a person thinks life is unfair and when they believe that God may be unfair is of utmost importance for the Pentecostal. That is not to say that emotions are rational in any way. Is God to blame for all the problems? Has the Most High somehow treated humanity in a manner that they did not deserve? These questions are complex, but the short answer is "probably not." Suppose the inclusion of the Psalms of Lament in scripture reveals something to their readers: that God wants people to be honest in our emotions with Him. We must have moments of what Walter Brueggemann calls orientation, disorientation, and new orientation.[67] These phases are weaved into each life; it is something that Brueggemann calls the "movement of our life, if we are attentive, is the movement of orientation, disorientation, and reorientation. And in our daily pilgrimage, we use much of our energy for this work."[68] If these movements are commonplace in every person's life, why do we as Christians in North America only feel that we can come to God during orientation or reorientation (new orientation)? Pentecostals only allow themselves to come to God in the disorientation phase when they are contrite for a sin committed. They do not allow their anger to factor into how they approach God, yet even Christ on the cross cried out emotionally, albeit not in anger, to the Father. His plea from the cross was akin to the cries of the various psalmists who asked, "How long?" However, we cannot remain in the accusatory tone; we must be willing to allow God to move us from the lament to the reorientation. Pentecostals then should modify their spiritual practices to include times of honest lament and to

---

66. Holladay, *The Psalms*, 269.
67. Brueggemann, *Spirituality of the Psalms*, 21.
68. Brueggemann, *The Psalms and the Life of Faith*, 24.

learn or perhaps relearn ways to incorporate the Psalms into their daily devotional life, to understand suffering in light of a theology of the cross, and also to give the Psalms the same respect which Luther did.

The Psalms, especially the lament psalms, are helpful as a personal praxis and valuable for pastoral care and counselling. Pastoral care has been inundated with secular ideas, which have replaced the theological roots of pastoral care.[69] However, if the Psalter is incorporated back into the practice of Pentecostals, in pastoral and self care they will be able to re-establish the theology which has been abandoned, to understand suffering in light of the cross. In the psalms, especially those of lament, one can better understand the grief process and free themselves from "obtrusive pious expectations and allow them to be angry with God."[70] The alternative is to internalize anger, which may not allow the practitioner to return to the worship of the Almighty. The lament psalms reveal the discordant petitioner eventually returns to the place of praise. Praise should be the natural ending point for all healthy grief and lament; that is not to say that lament and grief ever entirely subside but that we adjust and reorient in our grief as "praising God is where despair and depression need to turn."[71]

Lament as a Spiritual Practice

There is an absence of the usage of lament in the Pentecostal church praxis. Yes, there is an allowance for grieving; however, it is often compartmentalized and put out of sight, save for the days surrounding the funeral. Lament has been relegated to the far corners of our private lives and downgraded from our corporate expression in worship. The church, as John Swinton declares, "remains in denial, excluding the reality of pain and evil."[72] Perhaps these are not easy things for the church and its clergy to come to terms with, as few people in our society have a penchant for embracing their pain. However, through lament, our suffering is given a voice, and by doing so we have the proper language to express our pain before God. Unexpressed moments of pain only serve to alienate us from the Trinity by building barriers and not seeking a resolution.

---

69. Ballard, "Use of Scripture," 165.
70. Ballard, "Use of Scripture," 166.
71. Brown and Schweitzer, "Psalms." 5.
72. Swinton, *Raging with Compassion*, 113.

On the other hand, expressed lament can spur "movement towards God at a time when natural instinct is to move away from God. Lament gives a voice to rage and releases us to experience God's compassion."[73] In modern Christian worship, a person expressing lament spiritually is seen as having less of a steady relationship with God, because they dare to question the divine. In the Pentecostal church, Christians would often be perceived as less spiritual if they uttered phrases similar to those of the Psalmists who penned the lament psalms. The cries to God of "how long" are no longer seen as appropriate in our worship settings. We have instead pushed the negative emotions into the corners of our life and out of the faith perspective. We do this because we are uncomfortable with negative and raw emotions and perhaps even intimidated by them.[74]

Instead, the church has placed an over-reliance upon professional counsellors and support groups as a tool for emotional recovery instead of using our faith setting; this is not to suggest that psychotherapy has no place in society, but perhaps it would be less needed if people felt the ability to be honest with God and other believers. Brueggemann states that "It may be suggested that the one-sided liturgical renewal of today has, in effect, driven the hurtful side of experience either into obscure corners of faith practice or completely out of Christian worship into various forms of psychotherapy and growth groups."[75]

Lament is not simply wishing bad circumstances would change. A lament is an act of crying out in faith to God. It is not neat and tidy; it is not an idyllic image but rather a messy and hellish picture of the realities of life as it is lived. It is in these moments which we cry out to God. In modern congregational settings, it is considered anathema to be accusatory towards God in our times of trouble, and yet this is a valid expression of lament, as seen in the scriptures. Drawing upon his practice within a more liturgical setting, Colin Buchanan writes that our lament may involve "crying out against God, of anger against God, of puzzlement–aporia–in the presence of God, but all expressions are done with the knowledge that God. . .is nevertheless there, and in liturgy being specifically addressed."[76] There must be a re-imagination of the usage of the spiritual practice of lament in the Christian life; this allows the Christian spiritual life to have the same ability

---

73. Swinton, *Raging with Compassion*, 113.
74. Brueggemann, *Life of Faith*, 70.
75. Brueggemann, *Life of Faith*, 68.
76. Buchanan, "Liturgy and Lament," 157.

to vent towards God that the Israelites had in the Psalms and other scriptures, where they could cry out to God with their questions, even when it seemed they were being accusatory towards God. There is a need in North American Christendom to recapture the ability to converse with God in a manner that is "vigorous, candid, and daring."[77] We need to recapture the use of emotions in worship, both positive and negative so that our worship may have depth. Unfortunately, we exclude emotions, especially those that are perceived as negative, and in doing so, we end up having services that "feel flat and dispassionate."[78] The task of implementing this reinsertion of the spiritual practice into the praxis of the congregation so that there is a renewed vibrancy in the congregational worship will fall largely on the shoulders of the clergy of the local congregation. According to Bonnie Miller-McLemore, pastoral theology has a strong legacy of "investigating human suffering and spiritual recovery, creating fresh theological loci such as pain, lament, and joy."[79] The pastor's responsibility then is to use the situations of life, including the pain and lament, to help develop the church into a fuller experience in their spirituality. A congregation whose praxis includes both corporate joy and corporate lament will have a spirituality that contains depth. There will be greater faith, greater hope, and greater love when the Christian is taught how to express lament as a proper spiritual endeavour. Waltke, et al. in discussing this absence of Lament from our churches say, that if "Pain — is missed — in Praise, as Emily Dickinson suggested, then as some pastoral theologians are now arguing, it is time we began to make more use of lament as a renewed focus for hope."[80]

While it is obvious that lament is a beneficial spiritual practice, the challenges in implementing congregational and personal lament in the Western church will be great. The pastoral theologian must somehow break the mindset of a Christianity that as was discussed earlier, to put off the shackles of the ideology that we are both exceptional and triumphal. Our society wants to cheer alongside the winners and not cry beside the losers, we embrace success but shun failure. Lament as a corporate worship practice is "vastly different from that of modern evangelical corporate worship, which tends to emphasize rejoicing and positive thinking."[81] If we are to

---

77. Brueggemann, *Spirituality of the Psalms*, 74.
78. Rognlien, *Experiential Worship*, 121.
79. Miller-McLemore, *Christian Theology*, 18.
80. Waltke, *The Psalms as Christian Lament*, 2.
81. Ahrens, "Suffering, Soul Care, and Community," 100.

incorporate lament as a practical tool in the spiritual development of the congregant in the average western evangelical church, then we must also find ways to reimagine our identity. As a society, we must move away from the concept that we are exemplary and immune to disaster and instead embrace the foibles and problems that come our way. We, however, do not embrace them to glorify them but as a reason to call deeply unto the Lord. We must use our times of affliction to attempt theological reflection, for it is in these times where God "removes one source of joy and meaning that we were counting on to make our lives worth living, and replaces it with nothing. God puts us in a box where all we have is him."[82] Without the distractions of a contented life, we are thrust into the decision to either run to God or run away as far as we possibly can. The discipline of corporate spiritual lament will allow us to come face to face with our failures and see them as an opportunity to embrace God.

As it stands now, our culture does not do well in admitting our failures, our trials, our pain, and our sorrow. Instead, we shove them into the recesses of our souls and seek more joy without ever confronting the problems. Making people understand that coming face to face with the "negative" will create a deeper spirituality in their lives will be a significant challenge. Utilizing the PRP method on a clergy and congregational level will aid the Pentecostal clergy and congregation to become more spiritually whole in times of joy and sorrow.

Lament as Praxis for Pentecostals

It would be insufficient to name the practice of lament as a corrective without providing detailed methods in which Pentecostal clergy members and their congregations could utilize it. I suggest there are four good ways to incorporate lament into Pentecostal praxis. These are lament as a form of prayer, lament as worship/song, the gift of tongues and lament, and lament as an expression of corporate grief. Each of these will be detailed further in the coming paragraphs.

Lament as prayer is utilized in Appendix 4 and provided as an outline for the person who wishes to practice lament. That appendix draws on one Psalm of lament to detail how we can utilize the biblical method of lament in our praxis. The Pentecostal puts great value on the usage of scripture in both praxis and theology, therefore, the utilization of prayers modelled after

82. Crabb, *The Safest Place*, 12–13.

the Psalms and other lament sections of scripture, and the actual recitation of those passages of biblical lament would be helpful. It would be beneficial for the Psalms to be reincorporated into the life of the Pentecostal church in Canada and the rest of Western Pentecostal expressions, not only for simple reading but for practical spiritual application, for in its pages, there is a wealth of practical spirituality and deep theological concepts that can be incorporated into both the individual lives and corporate lives of believers. The Psalter should not be viewed as just another book contained in the scriptures, but it should be viewed as containing transformative qualities as we read and incorporate it into church life and praxis. The Psalter will help the believer to discover the patterns and purposes of their lives. The Psalms are rich with the concept of waiting on God to discover these things.[83] The person who utilizes lament into their praxis is incorporating a rich practice with its foundations firmly entrenched in the biblical account.

Additionally, the usage of the gift of tongues for the Pentecostal can be utilized as a form of lament. In discussing Gordon Fee's writings, Stephen Torr summarizes that there are "grounds for arguing for a pneumatological aid in the performance of lament, but specifically, one can propose that it is possible, particularly when one does not know what to pray, that the Spirit aids a fitting performance by enabling lament in the form of glossolalia."[84] This "groaning in the Spirit" is a praxis which Pentecostals already utilize and therefore to show it as a part of lament in prayer will aid them in also incorporating lament outside of the usage of glossolalia.

The second practical application is to utilize lament in both personal and corporate worship. Walter Brueggemann postulates that "a church that goes on singing 'happy songs' in the face of raw reality is doing something very different from what the Bible itself does."[85] Swinton comments that in small group settings, it would be appropriate to start writing songs of lament so that the community can better express its feelings in ways that are "rich and appropriate."[86] Pentecostals could also utilize songs from Christendom throughout the ages which provide language rich in lament in both a corporate and individual setting.

The final practical application would be that the Pentecostals have corporate lament times. This can come by looking to other sects within

---

83. Nouwen, *Discernment*, 151.
84. Torr, *Dramatic*, 194.
85. Brueggemann, *Message of the Psalms*, 52.
86. Swinton, *Raging with Compassion*, 127.

Christendom who utilize lament as a common practice in order that they may utilize these when appropriate. For example, they could borrow the idea of burying the alleluias during Lent from some more liturgical sects so that there can be an extended yearly time for corporate lament. Admittedly, this will be hard to implement in a Pentecostal church setting as there tends to be a distrust of liturgical acts of worship. However, if Pentecostals are shown that this can be a way to experience God and is not just a cold, religious performance, they will be more open to the concept. In addition, Torr suggests accepting a corporate ideal of lament in the Pentecostal churches would be for the clergy to lead their congregation in lament and crying out during devastation such as 9/11, natural disasters, or other highly traumatic events. He believes this would introduce lament in a practical way, which would allow for a slow introduction to the concept with an issue that is father away from them geographically and emotionally, which will not "place the same amount of strain on the theology of those lamenting as crying out over an issue closer to home perhaps would."[87]

The Way Forward According to Interview Subjects

Phenomenology looks to understand the essences of the matter being studied, in this case, how clergy experience trauma; it does not seek to ask interview subjects their ideas on how to fix their problems, whether perceived or otherwise. The interviews never sought the opinions of the subjects so if an opinion was given, it was unsolicited and not every subject provided one. However, this section will briefly share the thoughts of the subjects who provided an opinion without providing extensive commentary on their thoughts.

Jackie comments that one of the deficiencies of Christian worship, especially Pentecostal worship, is an "absence of songs of lament." She continues that we need to know how to "encounter God in suffering not just in good times."

Andrew suggests that the Pentecostal praxis would benefit from incorporating a communal idea of mourning. He says that while "we may not have all the answers just being present and just, you know, renting our own clothes and pouring in the ashes on our heads and just sitting with someone mourning."

---

87. Torr, *Dramatic*, 218.

Danny, on the other hand, says he has come to realize that he can not always be the "answer guy" and that instead, he has to "point people to Jesus. And I don't want to get down in the weeds. I want to, I want to keep people's eyes fixed on him, but it's tough, man."

Connie found some help in seeking counselling during her trauma when she felt that God had abandoned her. During counselling, she realized that she was "just going through the motions. It would be better if I just screamed at God instead of having this coldness."

Kirk suggested that for him, the solution was to be in relationship with other people who could empathize with his suffering. He says that "the pastor needs to feel comfortable by feeling he is in relationship" where they can share their trials.

Will suggests that there is a lack of resources in the denomination for clergy who are suffering, and that a possible solution would be if "there were resources provided by the head office."

Shawn feels that the solution is to show the sufferer that "somebody is there to care and love on them. And it's not just about telling me that God's got it all worked out." Essentially, he was saying something similar to Kirk's suggestion of a communal approach to handling suffering in the Christian community.

Mark, who suggested during his interview that he felt like damaged goods because of his trauma, believes that we need to realize as clergy that everyone experiences trauma, and we must stop "treating each other like damaged goods." He associated his trauma with people stigmatizing him, and thinks the solution in part is to recognize the prevalence of trauma and take a sympathetic approach.

Finally, Les thinks that leadership in the Pentecostal church would be wise to understand that clergy feel abused by "leadership within the church, and systems should be put in place to better deal with it."

SUMMARY

This chapter has utilized Osmer's normative and pragmatic tasks through theological reflection. A discussion has taken place regarding Pentecostal triumphalism, its history, its theological roots, and its problems; this was done by utilizing Pentecostal theologians who realized that the existing approach is deficient. Theologians such as Frank Macchia, David Courey, Martin Mittelstadt, and others revealed room for suffering in our theology and praxis, and some even suggested looking at Luther's *theologia crucis* as a conversation partner for Pentecostals. Luther's works were brought into the conversation to better understand what the theology of the cross would mean for Pentecostals. Since theology also needs to be a lived experience, the final section of this chapter suggested that utilizing a practice of lament would be a perfect avenue to combine the theology of the cross with our own experiences in praxis. In the final chapter, a discussion takes place sharing areas of future research and limitations of the current study.

6

Conclusion

WHAT MOTIVATES A PERSON to study trauma? Since practical theology and practice-led research seek to answer questions rooted in practice, the motivation for this project comes from my own experience. Not only have I experienced trauma through my son's death, but there have also been times when trauma was significant in my life. My parent's divorce as a child, my second daughter's illness, bullying within the church, job loss, and many other things have caused me to feel the effects of trauma in my life. Additionally, I have experienced vicarious trauma through the lives of my congregants; I have had to sit beside parents whose daughter had died, and I have been in the hospital when a person was given a grim diagnosis. All these things caused me to question where God was in all of this, and I realized I did not have an appropriate means to understand these situations, given my theology and praxis. As this study concludes, the coming pages summarize the findings of the research and the steps forward. It then discusses the study's limitations and areas of possible future research.

It should be noted that I entered this research with the presupposition that Pentecostals would benefit from incorporating both Luther's *theologia crucis* into their theology and also adding a practice of lament to their praxis. These presuppositions arose from my experience with trauma and suffering as I felt there was an inadequacy in my understanding of the Pentecostal theology I was taught and the praxis provided in the Pentecostal churches I was familiar with. Even though I had these presuppositions, I was not anchored to them in a concrete way; I was willing to allow the research to move my conclusions in a different direction. However, after completing the phenomenological interviews and the literature review, especially the areas surrounding Pentecostal theology, my presuppositions were justified.

THE PROBLEM

Since clergy are caregivers and often hear the needs and traumas of others, this places them in the position of being recipients of vicarious trauma. Vicarious trauma occurs when the caregiver is inundated with the trauma of others and takes that trauma as their own. Additionally, clergy also experience personal traumatic events, including but not limited to death, emotional and physical abuse, fear of safety, and a myriad of other issues. Clergy are invited into lives at the "most profound, painful, and meaningful moments, and no two situations are the same. Thus, clergy members and faith leaders are asked to be skilled in a multitude of situations and circumstances when stakes are high."[1] As a member of the clergy, I have been called to the bed of a dying child and celebrated another child's birthday within a few hours, all while struggling to cope with my internal issues. To be called to the highs and lows of a person's life and having personal struggles is common amongst the clergy.

The Solution

This section will briefly discuss the discoveries which were gained through the interviews, the theological interaction with trauma, and then restate the proposal of the study, which is for Pentecostals to incorporate Luther's *theologia crucis* into their theology and, through that, utilize a more profound understanding to the practice of lament.[2]

Interview Discoveries

Seven primary essences of clergy trauma were uncovered during the interviews. The first essence was that the clergy felt heightened anxiety during

---

1. Roozeboom, *Neuroplasticity*, 52.
2. For a concise representation of the essences which were discovered during the interviews please see the chart on pages 105–106.

CONCLUSION

their traumatic response. These were manifested physically through symptoms such as heart palpitations, loss of breath, angry outbursts, impatience, and various other ways. Internally the subjects suggested that uncertainty about the future or heightened awareness of danger were significant expressions of this essence.

Second, the subjects relayed that a sense of loneliness often accompanied the trauma. Some subjects said a sense of loneliness related to ministry already existed, but their trauma exacerbated the feelings. Loneliness led to them feeling that they had nowhere to turn for spiritual help and no one in whom to confide. Also associated with loneliness was the feeling of rejection, primarily if the clergy's trauma was related to a church conflict.

Third, a key finding in this research, which differed from secular studies which were not faith-focused, was that there was a tendency among participants to either question why God would allow the trauma to happen or they would become angry with God. Sometimes, this anger also contributed to a sense of guilt because they felt they should not be accusatory towards God. Other times, guilt manifested because the person believed they must have done something wrong. With this essence was the question of whether God still loved them or was their experience signifying that He had abandoned them. The study showed that for some participants, this feeling caused them to withdraw from God for extended periods.

Fourth, a high representation of the clergy who participated in the study expressed that they felt unsupported by leadership during their trauma; this could be either denominational leadership, local church leadership, or other leaders around them. In some cases, the clergy felt leadership took an adversarial role against them.

Fifth is self-doubt, which I refer to as a predator which pushes deep into a person's psyche. This essence was expressed in various ways, from deep self-loathing to questioning their abilities or whether they were fit to be a clergy member. In addition, self-doubt manifested as extreme embarrassment over their traumatic situation and gave them a warped sense of personal responsibility where the sufferer thought everything was their fault.

The sixth essence, brain fog, was expressed as an essence in many of the interviews. It was revealed in four primary ways, first as confusing thoughts where the sufferer became easily confused. Second, it made it difficult for them to distinguish reality from fantasy; they would feel like they were in a dream. The third way was a lack of focus; they could not pay attention to their tasks. Finally, they did not understand what was going on.

Seventh, during their traumatic experiences, the clergy often felt that they were disempowered. In some cases, disempowerment was caused by people belittling them or by perceived intimidation. In addition, some participants began to feel helpless and lacked personal power during their trauma because they could not fix the situation.

Five other findings were revealed during the analysis of the phenomenological interviews in relation to their spiritual practices. First, there was a frequency change in the spiritual practices during and after trauma. While some participants shared that they never stopped their spiritual practices, others indicated an increase or decrease in the duration they had. Second, the intensity of the spiritual practices increased for many, even for some who said the frequency of their spiritual practices decreased. The third item is that some participants developed new spiritual practices during and after trauma; some revealed they did this to "find out which one will work." Fourth, a few of the participants volunteered that they felt there was no place for suffering in Pentecostal theology and praxis; this was not a question which was asked of the participants, so the revelation of this item is significant. Finally, one participant brought up the theological perspective that they felt they were suffering with Christ during their trauma. Again, this was not directly asked of the participants, but since this is a crucial idea behind Luther's *theologia crucis* it is worthy of mention here.

Theological Interaction with Trauma

Examination of trauma studies foregrounds the sociological framework of the study. It was revealed in the literature review that 70 percent of the population of the United States had experienced trauma, and 76.1 percent of Canadians over eighteen have had at least one traumatic event in their lifetime. With those numbers in mind, it can be said that trauma is a common occurrence in North America; this highlighted the importance of this area of study.

Within trauma, there are four specific types: acute trauma caused by one significant event. Second, chronic trauma is typified by ongoing events, such as bullying, racism, or similar occurrences. Vicarious trauma is the third type; it often occurs to caregivers and people in fields which provide care for people, such as first responders and clergy; this trauma happens when the person caring for another takes on the trauma of the person for whom they are caring. The last type is post-trauma syndromes, such as PTSD. This area

Conclusion

of trauma was excluded from this study due to ethical concerns established during the McMaster Research Ethics Board approval process.

The literature review also revealed that trauma is not the event but rather the "specific and automatic collection of physiological responses to an event, which are triggered when an individual's or community's adaptive capacity is overwhelmed."[3] It is not the death of a loved one that is the trauma; our reaction to that event is the traumatic response. Trauma renders the afflicted powerless, as they are overwhelmed by their body's reactions through both automatic physiological responses and learned behaviour from past trauma. The responses to trauma may occur through external and internal physical symptoms such as emotional outbursts, anxiety, edginess, loss of appetite, inability to sleep, high blood pressure, heart palpitations, sweating, loss of breath, or various other ways. The people who experience trauma often tell highly charged emotional stories, which we also saw during the phenomenological section of this study. The phenomenological study also revealed that the clergy who participated were affected by all three types of trauma under study.

The literature review and theological reflection showed that the Pentecostal theology within the PAOC and PAONL leans towards a triumphalistic attitude; this partially occurs because Pentecostals were highly influenced by their holiness movement roots which brought with them the underlying Arminian and Methodist perfectionist motifs. These perfectionist motifs bring optimism to their movement, enabling them to view it as an end-time restoration of Pentecost to the church. The literature review and the theological reflection on the phenomenological study further revealed that Pentecostals have a sense of exceptionalism; they view themselves as being on a mission from God, against which no force can stand. These concepts emerge from their Christology, which declares that Jesus is healer and that Jesus is soon coming King. Additionally, the conceptual framework that Pentecostals hold regarding the enduement of power and an eschatological connection brings with it the idea that they are the ones who are helping to usher in the last days, as seen in Joel 2:28. By embracing the power narrative, it leads the Pentecostals to a sense of triumphalism which we see David Courey regard as an "embrace of the entire victory of the resurrected Christ with little recognition of the worlds of tensions and ambiguities in which the church is called to offer her witness."[4] With the general sense of

---

3. Ison, "Embodied and Systemic," 1.
4. Courey, *What Has Wittenberg*, 7.

triumphalism in Pentecostalism, the clergy who face the darker side of life have no tools or existing beliefs to turn to when the darkness prevails. They turn either to blaming Satan or otherworldly sources for their struggles, blaming themselves for not measuring up to God's requirements or in guilt, questioning God. The first item can lead to a crisis of faith when their power motif fails to provide relief over what they view as a demonic attack. The second item manifests self-doubt and questioning who they are in faith, which can lead to questioning their calling to ministry. Blaming God, the third item we have seen from the literature review and the phenomenological studies, can lead to a heightened sense of guilt. All of these can lead clergy persons to pull away from God in their praxis.

Proposal

The literature review and theological reflection established that Pentecostals hold a triumphalistic theology and have no avenue in which to turn when trauma persists; a corrective theology was suggested in Luther's *theologia crucis*. Luther believed in the supernatural, making him someone Pentecostals could sympathize with. He believed that Satan was active in the world, which affected us and those around us. In addition, he never forbade the usage of the charismata but just urged caution in their usage. This coherence between the two allows the Pentecostals to hold to their underlying theology while adding the *theologia crucis*. In the theology of the cross, we see that Luther suggests that there is an emptying of self during suffering, which allows God to work deeper in that person. The literature review highlighted six ways Pentecostal theologian Kärkkäinen believes Luther's *theologia crucis* would best be implemented in theology and praxis. Those will not be restated, but it would be wise for the Pentecostals to continue to familiarize themselves with these suggestions as they are helpful.

Through the implementation of the theology of the cross, Pentecostals will also be able to establish a practice of lament so that they may better experience Christ in their suffering. To do this would answer the question of Osmer's fourth task, where we are called to ask, "How might we respond?" The research asked, "How can a Pentecostal who holds a triumphalistic theology react when trauma persists?" The answer, in part, was that they ought to incorporate a new theological lens to better view suffering in a multifaceted way instead of how they currently do. The lens suggested was that Luther's *theologia crucis* would be a perfect addition to Pentecostal

CONCLUSION

theology. However, there must also be a praxis which accompanies this theology when the dark side of life persists. Pentecostals would be well served by incorporating the practice of lament into their praxis. They must call upon the works of Luther, Walter Brueggemann, John Patton, and others to verify that it is not only a scriptural response to suffering but also a historically Christian one as well.[5]

Limitations and Areas for Future Research

This section will discuss the limitations of this study, followed by areas for future research. Van Manen suggests there is no bottom to the findings in phenomenological research. Another person can take up a study on the same phenomenon and have new essences reveal themselves in the study. That is to say, this study should not be viewed as all-encompassing in nature when revealing the essences of clergy trauma. A second limitation is that the people interviewed in this study were primarily self-diagnosed as having trauma; while some were clinically diagnosed, the majority were not. This may mean that some were not suffering from actual trauma. However, considering the rates of trauma in Canada, there is high confidence in the study and the participants. Third, this study only utilized people who experienced trauma while in ministry; in some cases, the trauma pre-existed but continued while in ministry, but never was there a case where the trauma was entirely prior to ministry; this does not allow for a significant look into how people who are already traumatized cope while in ministry. Finally, this study only examined Pentecostal clergy; a study of other denominations would be helpful for future studies however, I believe there are many correlations between Pentecostals and the larger Evangelical community in many of the topics discussed.

Additionally, we could also look at the effects of trauma on congregants, children and spouses of clergy, and many other subgroups to obtain a better understanding of how trauma affects church life.

---

5. Pentecostals hold in high regard scripture, showing that the practice of lament is rooted in scripture will help them to come to terms with utilizing a methodology which sometimes might cry out against God. A worksheet based on Psalms 13 is provided in Appendix 4 to guide people in starting the practice of lament.

Concluding Statements

It is of hope that this study will provide further resources in academia but also provide resources to clergy in the midst of trauma. So that both the academy and the pastor in the pulpit will understand that their suffering is a typical experience, it is possible to develop deeper spiritual interactions through a theology of the cross and the practice of lament.

Appendix One
List of Essences and Spiritual Practices[1]

Code System	Code	Frequency
Code System	Code	557
	T- Sermons/Podcasts	3
	T-Job	1
	T-Volunteering	1
	T-Attend Church	1
	T-Family Devotions	2
	T - Worship Music	2
	T - Journaling	2
	T - Reading	4
	T - Devotional	4
	T - Connect with People / Christian Leaders	3
	T - Thanking God for Blessings	1
	T - Medatative/Listening	6
	A - To Deal with Trauma be prepared Spiritually	1
	T- Prayer	14
	T-Bible	10
	protective of one who caused trauma	10
	Emotional detachment	5
	develop boundaries /Aware of surroundings	9
	Anxiety / Stress	35
	self doubt / loathing / guilt	25
	Physiological Symptoms	15

1. Codes with THEO in front of it was noted when the person made a theological statement. T denotes a typical spiritual practice before trauma, whereas A denotes spiritual practice after trauma. All other codes with no prefix are the essences of trauma as described by the person.

APPENDIX ONE

Loneliness / Isolated	27
Authority - Unsupportive/Loss of respect of	43
Injustice	8
Negatively Impacted view of Church/Christians/God (+)	2
self concious / embarrassed	3
Feeling of Impending Doom	6
helpless / Loss of Control	10
Numbness (Life, Spirituality, Relationships)	14
Uncertian Future / Identity	8
Protective of others	15
Brain Fog / Disassociation / Confusion	21
Questioning or Anger towards God	29
Lack or Loss of Community / Rejected	15
Trust Issues	7
hurt / betrayed	10
abused / threatened	5
Shock / Speechless	7
manipulated / taken advantage of	2
Ongoing Bodily memories	7

Appendix Two
Interview Guide

INFORMATION ABOUT THESE INTERVIEW questions: These interviews are designed to gather clear descriptions of your own experiences with trauma and how it may have affected your spiritual practices. I will give you open-ended questions to help guide your thinking. Sometimes I will use other short questions to make sure I understand what you told me or if I need more information when we are talking such as: "So, you are saying that . . .?," to get more information "Please tell me more?," or to learn what you think or feel about something "Why do you think that is. . .?." As you answer the questions, please remember that you are free to skip any questions that make you feel uncomfortable or that you do not wish to answer.

There are three types of trauma.

- Acute trauma results from a single incident. (such as rape, a car accident, natural disaster.)
- Chronic trauma is repeated and prolonged such as domestic violence or abuse (physical, emotional, or otherwise).
- Complex trauma is exposure to varied and multiple traumatic events, often of an invasive, interpersonal nature. (such as neglect)

As the participant, you should be aware that in the event that the research uncovers activities that would require legal or medical disclosure, the researcher is obligated to contact the proper authorities.

1. Information about you:
   - Your age now?
   - Marital status.

APPENDIX TWO

- Ethnicity.
- Who lives with you in your home?
- How long have you been in Pastoral ministry?

2. Please tell me what your usual spiritual practices are each day.
3. Please share with me a specific experience in which you have experienced trauma, please be as detailed as possible.

    - Describe the experience as you lived it.
    - What especially stands out for you—what is vivid in your mind?
    - How did you feel at the time—what was happening inside you—bodily experiences, mood, emotions... what did it feel like?
    - Who was present during the experience?
    - What did you say during the experience?
    - Other prompts:
        - Who said what?
        - How did you feel about that?
        - In what way?
        - Can you give me an example?
        - What was it like to....?

4. Did the trauma affect how you practice your spirituality?

    - Did it affect how much you pray, worship, etc?
    - Did it affect your feelings about God?
    - Did it affect your feelings about another person?

5. Is there something important we forgot to explore?
6. Is there anything else you think I need to know about pastoral trauma and how it relates to their spiritual practices??

Appendix Three
McMaster Research Ethics Board

McMaster Research Ethics Board

November 2, 2021

Supervisor: Dr. Gordon Heath
Student Principal Investigator: Mr. Dale Sanger
Applicant: Dale Sanger
Project Title: Developing a Healthy Pastoral Spirituality when Facing Trauma
MREB#: 5426

Dear Researchers,

Thank you for sending me your response. Your careful attention to addressing, and documenting your responses to, all of the comments is greatly appreciated. Your clarifications and revisions address the majority of the prior concerns that were raised (but see conditions for clearance below). As such, I am approving your research protocol for ethics clearance. A certificate of clearance will be issued shortly. However, please note the following two conditions associated with your ethics clearance. Rather than asking you to go through another round of revisions and resubmission, as I understand that you wish to commence with data collection ASAP, I am instead granting you conditional clearance, and asking you to make the following changes to your recruitment script and LOI, prior to commencing with recruitment and data collection. Additionally, as soon as possible (but this need not happen prior to data collection), so that we have the MREB-approved versions of the below two documents attached to your protocol, please submit a "For Information Only" sub-form and upload the final versions of these documents. This form can be found by clicking on your study in Macrem, then "create sub-form", then select the FIO document -- hopefully this should only take you a couple of minutes.

1) <u>Email script sent from holder of participant contact info.</u>

   The email script that you have uploaded here appears to be identical to your email script that you will send directly to participants, and it reads as though it is coming from you, as opposed to coming from a participant (e.g. the first line states "Hello, I'm Dale Sanger.")

   Please add a line or two at the start of this script that says something like the following (using language that you prefer):

   "Hello, I'm contacting you on behalf of Dale Sanger, a graduate student at Divinity College, McMaster University, who has asked me to pass on to you the message below to tell you about a study he is conducting on [X]. Please see the attached letter of information and contact Dale if you have any further questions or are interested in participating."

2) <u>Letter of Information and Consent Form, Procedures involved in the research and/or Risks section:</u>

   Please also mention the wellness check follow-up call.

If this project includes planned in-person contact with research participants, then procedures for addressing COVID-19 related risks must be addressed according to the current processes communicated by the Vice-President (Research) and your Associate Dean (Research). All necessary approvals must be secured before in-person contact with research participants can take place.

All the best in your research.

Dr. Sue Becker

Dr. Violetta Igneski, MREB Chair,	**Dr. Sue Becker, MREB Vice-Chair,**
Associate Professor,	Professor,
Department of Philosophy, UH-308,	Department of Psychology, Neuroscience and Behaviour, PC-312,
ext. 23462,	ext. 23020,
igneski@mcmaster.ca	beckers@mcmaster.ca

Appendix Four
Lament Worksheet—Psalms 13

THIS WORKSHEET WILL PROVIDE an example of how to due Biblical lament using Psalms 13 as a guide.

PSALMS 13	
How long, O Lord? Will you forget me forever? How long will you hide your face from me? How long must I take counsel in my soul and have sorrow in my heart all the day? How long shall my enemy be exalted over me? (1-2)	Declare the Problem
Look on me and answer, Lord my God. Give light to my eyes, or I will sleep in death, and my enemy will say, "I have overcome him," and my foes will rejoice when I fall. (3-4)	State your Plea
But I trust in your unfailing love; my heart rejoices in your salvation. (5)	Praise God
I will sing the LORD's praise, for he has been good to me. (6)	Vow to God

Appendix Four

Do not rush through the steps. Take the time to write down your prayer as you complete each step. Follow the example of the Psalm until you become more comfortable using your own wording. Be specific, and endeavour to have God draw near to you during the process. Feel free to add to it every day you use it as new thoughts about your lament bubble to the surface. This exercise is not a solution to the problem which is causing your lament, your problem may go unresolved, but this exercise allows the participant to share honestly before God in prayer.

Bibliography

Ahrens, Ann Marie. "Suffering, Soul Care, and Community: The Place of Corporate Lament in Evangelical Worship." PhD diss., Southern Baptist Theological Seminary, 2017.
Akerlund, Truls. *A Phenomenology of Pentecostal Leadership*. Eugene, OR: Wipf & Stock, 2018.
Allain-Chapman, Justine. *Resilient Pastors: The Role of Adversity in Healing and Growth*. London: SPCK, 2013.
American Psychiatric Association, and American Psychiatric Association, eds. *Diagnostic and Statistical Manual of Mental Disorders*. 5th ed. Washington, D.C: American Psychiatric Association, 2013.
Anderson, Robert Mapes. *Vision of the Disinherited: The Making of American Pentecostalism*. Peabody, MA: Hendrickson, 1992.
Ballard, Paul. "The Use of Scripture." In *The Wiley-Blackwell Companion to Practical Theology*, edited by Bonnie J. Miller-McLemore, 163–72. Malden, MA: Wiley-Blackwell, 2012.
Bartleman, Frank. *How Pentecost Came to Los Angeles: As It Was in the Beginning*. 2nd ed. Self-Published, Frank Bartleman, 1925.
Brown, William P., and Carol L. Schnabl Schweitzer. "Psalms as Resources for Pastoral Care." In *The Oxford Handbook of the Psalms*, edited by William P. Brown. Oxford: Oxford University Press, 2014.
Brueggemann, Walter. *The Message of the Psalms: A Theological Commentary*. Augsburg Old Testament Studies. Minneapolis: Augsburg, 1984.
———. *The Psalms and the Life of Faith*. Minneapolis: Fortress Press, 1995.
———. *Spirituality of the Psalms*. Minneapolis: Fortress Press, 2002.
Buchanan, Colin. "Liturgy and Lament." In *Spiritual Complaint: The Theology and Practice of Lament*, edited by Miriam J. Bier and Tim Bulkeley. Eugene, OR: Pickwick, 2013.
Cahalan, Kathleen A., and James R. Nieman. "Mapping the Field of Practical Theology." In *For Life Abundant: Practical Theology, Theological Education, and Christian Ministry*, edited by Dorothy C. Bass and Craig R. Dykstra, 62–86. Grand Rapids: Eerdmans, 2008.

BIBLIOGRAPHY

Campbell, Eilidh. "Glory in Suffering? A Reflection on Finding Meaning in Grief through an Interrogation into the Phenomenology of Suffering." *Practical Theology* 13 (2020) 517–28. DOI: 10.1080/1756073X.2019.1707458.

Candy, Linda. *Practice Based Research: A Guide*. Sydney: Creativity & Cognition Studios, 2006. http://www.creativityandcognition.com/resources/PBR%20Guide-1.1-2006.pdf.

Conti, Paul. *Trauma: The Invisible Epidemic: How Trauma Works and How We Can Heal from It*. Boulder, CO: Sounds True, 2021.

Courey, David. *What Has Wittenberg to Do with Azusa? Luther's Theology of the Cross and Pentecostal Triumphalism*. London: T. & T. Clark, 2015.

Crabb, Larry. *The Safest Place on Earth: Where People Connect and Are Forever Changed*. Nashville, TN: Thomas Nelson, 2007.

Creswell, John W., and Cheryl N. Poth. *Qualitative Inquiry and Research Design: Choosing Among Five Approaches*. 4th ed. Los Angeles: SAGE, 2018.

Dayton, Donald W. *Theological Roots of Pentecostalism*. Grand Rapids: Baker Academic, 2011.

Engelbert, Pamela F. *Who Is Present in Absence: A Pentecostal Theological Praxis of Suffering and Healing*. Eugene, OR: Pickwick, 2019.

Eyer, Richard C. *Pastoral Care under the Cross: God in the Midst of Suffering*. St. Louis, MO: Concordia, 1994.

Ferguson, Neil. "Practice-Led Theology or Thinking Theology through Practice." PhD diss., University of Notre Dame Australia, 2014.

Forde, Gerhard O., and Martin Luther. *On Being a Theologian of the Cross: Reflections on Luther's Heidelberg Disputation, 1518*. Grand Rapids: Eerdmans, 1997.

Gornold-Smith, Christopher. "Spiritual Gifts in a Postmodern World: The Word of Wisdom, the Word of Knowledge, the Discerning Spirits." In *Pentecostal Gifts and Ministries in a Postmodern Era*, 19–46. Springfield, MO: Gospel Pub. House, 2004.

Gray, Carole. "Inquiry through Practice: Developing Appropriate Research Strategies." In *No Guru, No Method? Discussion on Art and Design Research*, edited by Pia Strandman, 1998. Reprint. http://carolegray.net/Papers%20PDFs/ngnm.pdf.

Grosch-Miller, Carla A. *Trauma and Pastoral Care: A Ministry Handbook*. London: Canterbury Press, 2021.

Herman, Judith Lewis. *Trauma and Recovery: The Aftermath of Violence; from Domestic Abuse to Political Terror*. New York: Basic Books, 2015.

Holladay, William Lee. *The Psalms through Three Thousand Years: Prayerbook of a Cloud of Witnesses*. Minneapolis: Fortress, 1993.

"How to Manage Trauma." National Council for Behavioral Health, [n.d]. https://www.thenationalcouncil.org/wp-content/uploads/2013/05/Trauma-infographic.pdf?daf=375ateTbd56.

Ison, Hilary. "Working with an Embodied and Systemic Approach to Trauma and Tragedy." In *Tragedies and Christian Congregations: The Practical Theology of Trauma*, 47–63. Explorations in Practical, Pastoral, and Empirical Theology. New York: Routledge, 2019.

Kärkkäinen, Veli-Matti. "Theology of the Cross: A Stumbling Block to Pentecostal/Charismatic Spirituality?" In *The Spirit and Spirituality: Essays in Honour of Russell P. Spittler*, edited by Wonsuk Ma et al., 150–63. Journal of Pentecostal Theology 24. New York: T. & T. Clark, 2004.

Bibliography

Keener, Craig S. *Spirit Hermeneutics: Reading Scripture in Light of Pentecost*. Grand Rapids: Eerdmans, 2017.

Klaus, Byron D. "Implications of Globalization for Pentecostal Leadership and Mission." In *Pentecostalism and Globalization: The Impact of Globalization on Pentecostal Theology and Ministry*, 127–150. McMaster Divinity College Press Theological Study Series 2. Eugene, OR: Pickwick, 2010.

Kwateng-Yeboah, James. "'Poverty Is of the Devil:' Pentecostal Worldviews and Development in Ghana." In *The Holy Spirit and Social Justice: Interdisciplinary Global Perspectives, History, Race and Culture*, edited by Antipas Harris and Michael Palmer, 180–207. Lanham, MD: Seymour, 2019.

Land, Steven J. *Pentecostal Spirituality: A Passion for the Kingdom*. Cleveland, TN: CPT Press, 2010.

Liebert, Elizabeth. *The Soul of Discernment: A Spiritual Practice for Communities and Institutions*. Louisville: Westminster John Knox, 2015.

Lloyd-Jones, D. Martyn. *Joy Unspeakable: Power and Renewal in the Holy Spirit*. Wheaton, IL: Shaw, 1985.

Luther, Martin. "Heidelberg Disputation (1518)," *Book of Concord*, [n.d.], https://bookofconcord.org/heidelberg.php.

Macchia, Frank D. *Baptized in the Spirit: A Global Pentecostal Theology*. Grand Rapids: Zondervan, 2009. EPub edition.

Melander, Rochelle. *Spiritual Leader's Guide to Self-Care*. Toronto: Rowman & Littlefield, 2002.

Menzies, William W., and Robert P. Menzies. *Spirit and Power: Foundation of Pentecostal Experience: A Call to Evangelical Dialogue*. Grand Rapids: Zondervan, 2000.

Miller, Thomas William. *Canadian Pentecostals: A History of the Pentecostal Assemblies of Canada*. Mississauga, ON: Full Gospel Pub. House, 1994.

Miller-McLemore, Bonnie J. *Christian Theology in Practice: Discovering a Discipline*. Grand Rapids: Eerdmans, 2012.

Mittelstadt, Martin William. *The Spirit and Suffering in Luke-Acts: Implications for a Pentecostal Pneumatology*. Journal of Pentecostal Theology 26. London: T. & T. Clark, 2004.

Neumann, Peter D. *Pentecostal Experience: An Ecumenical Encounter*. Princeton Theological Monograph Series 187. Eugene, OR: Pickwick, 2012.

Ngien, Dennis. *Fruit for the Soul: Luther on the Lament Psalms*. Minneapolis: Fortress, 2015.

Nouwen, Henri J. M. *Discernment: Reading the Signs of Daily Life*. New York: HarperOne, 2013.

Oberman, Heiko A. *Luther: Man between God and the Devil*. New York: Doubleday, 1992.

"The Old–Time Pentecost." The Apostolic Faith, September 1906.

Osmer, Richard. *Practical Theology: An Introduction*. Grand Rapids: Eerdmans, 2008.

PAOC Fellowship Stats. Statistics Pentecostal Assemblies of Canada, 2022, Online: https://paoc.org/docs/default-source/fellowship-services-documents/fellowship-stats-2022-at-19-jan-22.pdf?sfvrsn=e0a1f36a_2.

Patton, John H. *From Ministry to Theology: Pastoral Action and Reflection*. Eugene, OR: Wipf & Stock, 1995.

Peoples, Katarzyna. *How to Write a Phenomenological Dissertation: A Step-by-Step Guide*. Los Angeles: SAGE, 2021.

Qualls, Joy Elizabeth Anderson. *God Forgive Us for Being Women: Rhetoric, Theology, and the Pentecostal Tradition*. Eugene, OR: Pickwick, 2018.

BIBLIOGRAPHY

Rah, Soong-Chan. "The American Church's Absence of Lament." *Sojourners*, October 24, 2013, https://sojo.net/articles/12-years-slave/american-churchs-absence-lament.

Reimer, Sam. "Pastoral Well-Being: Findings from the Canadian Evangelical Churches Study." Church and Faith Trends 3 (2010) 1–17.

Richie, Tony. *Essentials of Pentecostal Theology: An Eternal and Unchanging Lord Powerfully Present and Active by the Holy Spirit*. Eugene, OR: Resource Publications, 2020.

Rognlien, Bob. *Experiential Worship: Encountering God with Heart, Soul, Mind, and Strength*. Colorado Springs, CO: NavPress, 2005.

Roozeboom, William D. *Neuroplasticity, Performativity, and Clergy Wellness: Neighbor Love as Self-Care*. Emerging Perspectives in Pastoral Theology and Care. Lanham: Lexington Books, 2017.

Satyavarata, Ivan. "Friends in Mission: Following the Wind and Riding the Wave." In *Pentecostalism and Globalization: The Impact of Globalization on Pentecostal Theology and Ministry*, 198–220. McMaster Divinity College Press Theological Study Series vol. 2. Eugene, OR: Pickwick, 2010.

Schiraldi, Glenn R. *Post-Traumatic Stress Disorder Sourcebook*. New York: McGraw-Hill, 2009.

Smail, Thomas Allan. "The Cross and the Spirit: Toward a Theology of Renewal." In *The Love of Power, or, The Power of Love: A Careful Assessment of the Problems within the Charismatic and Word-of-Faith Movements*, edited by Thomas Allan Smail et al., 13–36. Minneapolis: Bethany House, 1994.

Swinton, John. *Finding Jesus in the Storm: The Spiritual Lives of Christians with Mental Health Challenges*. Grand Rapids: Eerdmans, 2020.

———. *Raging with Compassion: Pastoral Responses to the Problem of Evil*. Grand Rapids: Eerdmans, 2018.

———. *Spirituality and Mental Health Care: Rediscovering a "Forgotten" Dimension*. London: Kingsley, 2001.

Swinton, John, and Harriet Mowat. *Practical Theology and Qualitative Research*. London: SCM, 2006.

Torr, Stephen C. *A Dramatic Pentecostal/Charismatic Anti-Theodicy: Improvising on a Divine Performance of Lament*. Eugene, OR: Pickwick, 2013.

Vaccarino, Franco, and Tony (Max Anthony) Gerritsen. "Exploring Clergy Self-Care: A New Zealand Study." *The International Journal of Religion and Spirituality in Society* 3 (2013) 69–80. DOI: 10.18848/2154-8633/CGP/v03i02/59264.

Van Ameringen, Michael, et al. "Post-Traumatic Stress Disorder in Canada." *CNS Neuroscience and Therapeutics* 14 (2008) 171–81. DOI: 10.1111/j.1755-5949.2008.00049.x.

Van der Kolk, Bessel A. *The Body Keeps the Score: Brain, Mind and Body in the Healing of Trauma*. New York: Penguin Books, 2015.

Van Manen, Max, et al. "A Conversation with Max van Manen on Phenomenology in Its Original Sense: Editorial." *Nursing and Health Sciences* 18 (2016) 4–7, DOI: 10.1111/nhs.12274.

———. "Phenomenology of Practice." *Phenomenology and Practice* 1 (2007) 11–30.

———. *Phenomenology of Practice: Meaning-Giving Methods in Phenomenological Research and Writing*. Walnut Creek, CA: Left Coast Press, 2014.

———. *Researching Lived Experience: Human Science for an Action Sensitive Pedagogy*. 2nd ed. London: Routledge, 2016.

Bibliography

———. "Serendipitous Insights and Kairos Playfulness." *Qualitative Inquiry* 24 (2018) 672–80, DOI: 10.1177/1077800418778714.

Waltke, Bruce K. *The Psalms as Christian Lament: A Historical Commentary*. Grand Rapids: Eerdmans, 2014.

Ward, Pete. *Introducing Practical Theology: Mission, Ministry, and the Life of the Church*. Grand Rapids: Baker Academic, 2017.

Watson, Essie. *Essie Watson to Walter McAlister*. PAOC National Archives. February 15, 1954.

Webb, Alan L. *So You Want to Do a Qualitative Dissertation?: A Step by Step Template That Will Guide You through a Qualitative Dissertation*. Self-published, Alan Webb, 2016.

Work, Telford. "Pentecostal and Charismatic Worship." In *The Oxford History of Christian Worship*. Oxford: Oxford University Press, 2006.

Zylla, Phil C. "Shades of Lament: Phenomenology, Theopoetics, and Pastoral Theology." *Pastoral Psychology* 63 (2014) 763–76. DOI: 10.1007/s11089-014-0616-2.

Index

Acute Trauma, 20–21
Ahrens, Ann Marie, 119
Akerlund, Truls, 12, 47
Allain-Chapman, Justine, 23–24
American Psychiatric Association, 4
Anderson, Robert Mapes, 33–34
Azusa Street Papers, 31

Ballard, Paul, 117
Bartleman, Frank, 99
Brown, William P., 117
Brueggemann, Walter, 9, 116, 118, 119, 121
Buchanan, Colin, 10, 118

Cahalan, Kathleen A., 8
Candy, Linda, 46
Campbell, Eilidh, 11, 43
Chand, Mineela, 5
Charcot, Jean-Martin, 3–4
Chronic Trauma, 21–22
Conti, Paul, 17, 18, 20, 21, 22
Courey, David, 8, 9, 30, 34, 35, 36, 37, 38, 39, 96, 97, 101, 105, 108, 111
Crabb, Larry, 120
Creswell, John W., 11, 47, 74

Data Gathering, 52–54, 55–57
Data Saturation, 63–64
Dayton, Donald W., 26, 27, 28, 29, 30, 33
Divine Healing, 30

Englebert. Pamela, 37, 107
Epoché, 48
Essences of Trauma, 56–57, 66–83
   anxiety, 67–69, 90, 126–127
   brain fog, 78–80, 91, 127
   disempowerment, 80–82, 92, 128
   loneliness, 69–71, 90–91, 127
   questioning/anger with God, 71–74, 91–92, 127
   self-doubt, 76–78, 93, 127
   unsupportive leadership, 74–75, 92, 127
Eyer, Richard C., 112

Ferguson, Neil, 7, 46
Forde, Gerhard, 108, 109, 110
Freud, Sigmund, 3–4

Gerritsen, Tony, 25
Gornold-Smith, Christopher, 99–100
Gray, Carole, 46
Grosch-Miller, Carla, 4, 5, 6, 19, 20, 22, 24

Herman, Judith, 4, 5, 17, 18, 19, 20, 21, 22, 23, 25
Holladay, William Lee, 116
Horseman, Sarah, 24
Human Function Curve, 24

Ison, Hilary, 7, 17, 26

James, William, 3

Index

Janet, Pierre, 3–4

Kärkkäinen, Veli-Matti, 30, 37, 39, 40, 106–107
Keener, Craig, 100–101
Klaus, Byron D., 102, 103
Kwateng-Yeboah, James, 97

Lament, 9–11, 88, 112–122, 125
Land, Steven J., 30, 33, 34, 35, 104, 105
Liebert, Elizabeth, 113
Lifeworld, 49–52
Lived Body, 50
Lived Other (relationality), 50
Lived Space (spatiality), 49
Lived Time, 50
Lloyd-Jones, D. Martyn, 31, 33, 36
Luther, Martin, 2, 9, 38, 39, 40, 108, 109, 110, 111

Macchia, Frank, 8, 100, 101, 103, 105
Melander, Rochelle, 25
Menzies, Robert, 32
Menzies, William, 32
Miller, Thomas William, 32
Miller-McLemore, Bonnie J., 10, 119
Mittelstadt, Martin William, 106
Mowat, Harriet, 13–14, 53
Myers, Charles, 4

Neumann, Peter, 32
Ngien, Dennis, 107, 110, 113–115
Nieman, James R., 8
Normative Task, 96
Nouwen, Henri, 121

Oberman, Heiko A., 97
Osmer, Richard, 44–45, 58, 94, 95

Participants, Description of, 54–55
Patton, John H., 115
Pentecostal Theology, 8–9, 26–37
Peoples, Katarzyna, 49
Power Evangelism, 31
Power Motifs in Holy Spirit Baptism, 29–33
Phenomenology, 11–14, 47–52

Post Trauma Syndromes, 23
Poth, Cheryl N., 11, 47, 74
Practical Theology, 6–8, 44–45
Practice-led Research, 6–8, 45–47
Pragmatic Task, 112–123

Qualls, Joy, 99

Rah, Soong-Chan, 9
Reduction, 48
Reimer, Sam, 22
Richie, Tony, 144
Rognlien, Bob, 119

Satyavarata, Ivan, 104
Schiraldi, Glenn R., 4, 20
Schweitzer, Carol, 117
Smail, Thomas Allen, 110
Soon Coming King, 33–35
Spiritual Practices, 83–87
Swinton, John, 10, 13–14, 26, 53, 117, 118, 121

Theologia Crucis (see Cross, Theology of)
Theology of the Cross, 2, 9, 16, 37, 38–41
   for Pentecostals, 108–112, 125
Torr, Stephen C., 31, 106, 121, 122
Trauma Studies, 3–9, 17–26
Triumphalism and Suffering, 16, 35–37, 96–108

Vaccarino, Franco, 25
Van Ameringen, Michael, 18
Van der Kolk, Bessel, 4, 6, 19, 21, 22, 26
Van Manen, Max, 11, 12, 13, 49, 50, 51, 52, 60, 61, 64, 66, 89
Vicarious Trauma (see Trauma Studies)
Vicarious Trauma, 22

Waltke, Bruce K., 119
Watson, Essie, 99
Ward, Pete, 45, 94
Webb, Alan L., 55, 64
Work, Telford, 102

Zylla, Phil, 11, 43

www.ingramcontent.com/pod-product-compliance
Lightning Source LLC
Chambersburg PA
CBHW060823190426
43197CB00038B/2207